CELEBRATE VEGAN

CELEBRATE VEGAN

200 Life-Affirming Recipes
for Occasions Big and Small

Dynise Balcavage

Guilford, Connecticut
An imprint of Globe Pequot Press

For the animals

To buy books in quantity for corporate use
or incentives, call **(800) 962–0973**
or e-mail **premiums@GlobePequot.com.**

Lyons Press is an imprint of Globe Pequot Press

Text design: Sheryl P. Kober
Project editor: Julie Marsh
Layout: Mary Ballachino

Library of Congress Cataloging-in-Publication Data is available on file.

ISBN 978-0-7627-7067-0

Printed in the United States of America

10 9 8 7 6 5 4 3 2 1

CONTENTS

INTRODUCTION
VEGAN IS A MOVEABLE FEAST

"Il faut des rites."
"Qu'est-ce qu'un rite?"
"C'est aussi quelque chose de trop oublié," dit le renard. "C'est ce qui fait qu'un jour est différent des autres jours, une heure, des autres heures."

Translation:
"We need rituals," said the fox.
"What's a ritual?" asked the little prince.
"It's something too easily forgotten," said the fox. "It's what makes one day different from the others, and one hour different from the other hours."
—from The Little Prince *by Antoine de Saint-Exupéry*

Holidays celebrate and reaffirm life. Since they help strengthen our bonds with family and friends—and with our religions, countries, and cultures—they also reinforce our identities. Holidays catapult us into syncopation: from the drudgery of everyday existence into full-blown celebration mode, heightening our senses and waking up our ability to experience joy.

Why not use holidays, both our own and those of other cultures, as a conduit to affirming life and to savoring and sharing its pleasures? Life, after all, should be a celebration. And vegan food certainly celebrates life in every sense of the word.

All this said, I think every day should be a holiday. Actually, if you consult a calendar—pick your poison: Julian, lunar, solar, Gregorian, Bahaist—practically every day is a holiday somewhere in the world. In this book, for example, I've included four entirely different New Year celebrations—New Year's, Nowruz (Persian New Year), Rosh Hashanah, and Chinese New Year—all of which fall on different days.

So please, prepare these recipes for all of life's parties and feasts—both big and small, both extraor-

dinary and ordinary. A chatty family supper can be a celebration. So can a meditative bowl of soup enjoyed alone, while simultaneously devouring a novel and listening to jazz.

It's important to keep in mind that most holiday recipes are based on history and stories of days gone by. What's interesting is that when you make these recipes, you continue the narrative. You become the storyteller. It's a magical time, when the past fuses with the present to lay the groundwork for the future.

We all have our favorite holidays. Pam, my oldest and "bestest" friend, loves Halloween so much that she chose it as her wedding day. My sister Babs and her daughters go gaga for Christmas. As for me, Thanksgiving is my holiday of choice. I love the concept of gratitude. Most of us have plenty to be grateful about—something you realize after spending any chunk of time with people in developing countries like India, or after undergoing or seeing someone you love undergo an illness. Still, most of us could use a little reminder. I also love the food and the fact that Thanksgiving's bounty is, for the most part, veg-centric.

NO HOLIDAY FOR FARM ANIMALS

Despite my love of Thanksgiving, honestly, it's always sad for me to sit at an omnivore's dinner table with a turkey corpse as the centerpiece. Bizarre, when you think about how immune most of us have become to dead flesh. Animals have almost become objectified to the point where meat no longer registers as something that, just a short time ago, was a sentient being that lived, ate, and slept, just as we do. Sadly, turkeys and other fowl are not protected under most state anticruelty laws. As a result, most live horrible lives in despicable conditions and then suffer unspeakable deaths.

I was in Jordan once, during Eid al-Fitr, the Islamic holiday that marks the end of the month-long fast of Ramadan (which, similar to Easter, breaks the forty days of fasting during Lent). It's a joyous, buzzing time. People dress up, exchange gifts, and enjoy the sumptuous foods with abandon. This holiday also focuses on the giving of alms—donating food or money to the poor. A common ritual is to slaughter a sheep and donate the meat to charity. On the morning of Eid, I saw at least ten fathers and their young sons slaughtering sheep and lambs. Devastating to witness, especially for a sensitive person like me. And from the looks on the little boys' faces, I don't think they liked it very much, either.

A CULINARY PARADIGM SHIFT: KINDER, GENTLER, HEALTHIER HOLIDAYS

Once you peek behind the curtain of animal cruelty, it's impossible to not speak up about it, through your actions, your words, or both. A culinary paradigm shift is long overdue. But if you're not used to a veg-centric diet, changing old habits and time-honored recipes can be stressful.

Major holidays like Christmas, Rosh Hashanah, and Ramadan are already stressful enough. We want our celebrations to be memorable and evolve into treasured family traditions. So we go all out, channeling our inner Martha Stewart, attempting to subscribe to some media-induced, unachievable ideal of kitchen god or goddess, instead of preparing simple, festive food that leaves us with enough time and energy left to actually—*gasp!*—enjoy the celebration. For vegans and vegetarians, this kind of stress tends to easily double because we feel anxious about our plant-based food being judged (or worse yet, ignored) by meat eaters.

It doesn't have to be this way. I wrote this book for several reasons:

- To provide flavorful vegan holiday recipes
- To motivate you to replace cruel holiday traditions with kind ones
- To inspire you to make every day a celebration and to learn to recognize and appreciate all the gifts and blessings in your lives

Bon appétit! And happy feasting.

VEGANIZING 101

As I wrote in my first cookbook, *The Urban Vegan,* I strongly dislike the verb "to veganize." It implies that omnivorous food is the holy grail of the culinary world. It insinuates that vegan food is inferior to omnivorous food and that we must attempt to replicate omnivorous recipes to make them match as closely as possible.

Nothing could be further from the truth. Vegan food is a fabulous culinary genre in its own right. But in the context of a book that centers on holiday and celebratory cooking, which, in turn, centers on many traditionally omnivorous foods, this verb is necessary, as are some specific instructions. Many of your non-vegan guests will be expecting traditional meat- and dairy-laden holiday dishes. And so yes, we will veganize. And yes, we will amaze.

MOCK MEATS

Many vegans and vegetarians shun mock meats on principle. I used to think it was admirable. Now, I think it's tiresome. If the only reason, for example, that a die-hard omnivore is not vegan or vegetarian is because he misses the taste of meat, then why shouldn't he be able to cook and purchase foods whose textures and flavors are similar to meat without fear of being ridiculed by fundamentalist vegangelicals? Plus, mock meats are improving in quality, and as a cook, it's nice to have an ever-expanding armamentarium of food items to experiment with. If you are a mock-meat fan, you're in luck because mo' better varieties are available; my local Whole Foods has an entire refrigerated case stocked with mock meat. Demand creates supply, people!

But mock meats are realtively expensive—and the highly processed foods used in some veg sausages and meats are not great for our health. For this reason, I don't indulge in veggie sausages and tenders often. I do, however, eat a lot of tofu, tempeh, and seitan. They are so easy to prepare and healthy, plus I love the chewy texture and protein pump they provide.

If you do buy mock meats, please read the labels. As with any food, ingredients should be simple, whole foods with pronounceable ingredients that you recognize.

You can generally swap equal amounts of vegan meats for meats in most recipes.

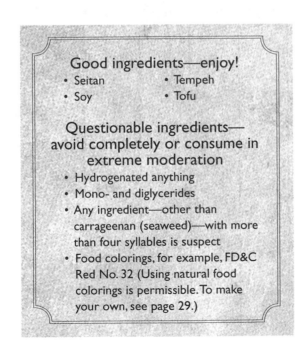

Good ingredients—enjoy!
- Seitan
- Tempeh
- Soy
- Tofu

Questionable ingredients— avoid completely or consume in extreme moderation
- Hydrogenated anything
- Mono- and diglycerides
- Any ingredient—other than carrageenan (seaweed)—with more than four syllables is suspect
- Food colorings, for example, FD&C Red No. 32 (Using natural food colorings is permissible. To make your own, see page 29.)

VEGAN CHEESES

Years ago, vegan cheeses used to be rubbery and have a synthetic flavor. Now, they are melty and tasty enough to fool any unknowing omnivore (which, I admit, I take great pleasure in doing from time to time). In fact, vegan cheeses have improved considerably since I wrote *The Urban Vegan* just two years ago, and they were pretty good even then. In Philadelphia, we now even have a vegan pizzeria called Blackbird that does a bustling business.

Daiya brand is my favorite vegan cheese. Like mock meats, vegan cheeses are expensive. So if you are going to splurge on cheese, you might as well opt for the cruelty-free, cholesterol-free versions, right? What a bargain! Sample a few varieties. You're bound to find something that pleases your palate. As is the case with mock meats, enjoy any processed vegan cheese in moderation.

By the way, vegan cheeses do not contain casein or whey, which are actually milk products. Some soy cheese does contain casein and/or whey, so be sure to check the label.

EGGS: THE BIGGEST BAKING MYTH

Whenever I do a cooking demo, the most popular question is inevitably, "How do you bake without eggs or milk?" Quite simply, eggs are not needed for baking. More people are realizing this, hence the proliferation of so many successful vegan bakeries around the country. (I was so stoked when the vegan baker impressed the socks off the judges on the Food Network's *Cupcake Wars* and actually won!) It's taken awhile to debunk this misconception—probably in part to the powerful farm and dairy lobbies—but it's finally happening.

Yes, adding eggs to batter is one way to give lift and moisture to baked goods. But if you dig a bit deeper, there are probably about ten other methods that accomplish the same end result—without adding cholesterol. In fact, many well-established vegan bakeries don't even use substitutes; they simply add more liquid, oil, and/or butter to make a moister cake.

EQUIPMENT NOTES:
KITCHEN EQUIPMENT THAT MAKES MY LIFE EASIER

It's no secret: I'm a sucker for Williams Sonoma, Sur La Table, and Kitchen Kapers. I can spend hours browsing in these stores and online, fantasizing about how I would equip my 500-square-foot dream kitchen. But life in a city loft—and common sense—prevents me from overindulging. When it comes to buying new kitchen equipment, I'm a brutal editor, first, because I don't have a lot of room, and second, because life is simpler when you own less stuff.

Procuring new kitchenware is an extremely personal choice. What's essential to me might not be essential to you, and vice versa. In some cases, new purchases do nothing but clutter up your junk drawers and provide fodder for your next yard sale. But other purchases can actually provide pleasure. Case in point: All my life, I simply boiled tea water in a saucepan. I had recently developed a penchant for drinking tea, and a few friends were surprised that I didn't own a tea kettle—and they teased me mercilessly about it. So I finally broke down and bought a cherry-red tea kettle, and hearing its comforting whistle has become an important component of my tea-making ritual. My quality of life has improved 300 percent, and I can't imagine how I did without it all these years.

Aside from my tea kettle, these items are time-savers and have enhanced my cooking experience.

Garlic press: I eat a lot of garlic, which adds up to a lot of chopping. With a garlic press, you simple place a whole clove inside the chamber, squeeze, and you have a nice pat of uniformly minced garlic. The peel stays inside the chamber; you simply remove it and toss it.

Good knives: For years, I struggled through my culinary adventures with cheap, crappy knives. Although I coveted better knives, I thought buying them was living beyond my means. Eventually, I broke down and bought a set of Henckels chef's knives, complete with butcher block storage unit, at a discounted price. I'm so glad I did. Unlike silly impulse purchase gadgets that clog up my drawers, these knives see daily use and make chopping so much easier. Get the best knives you can afford, and make sure they feel good in your hand.

Immersion blender: One day, I made red beet soup and decided to puree it in my blender. I filled the pitcher too full and the soup splattered all over my white walls, counters, and appliances. My kitchen looked like a murder scene. The following week, I bought an immersion blender. I haven't looked back.

Potato ricer: I'm surprised at how many people have never used a ricer; once you buy one, you'll find yourself making mashed potatoes at least once a week. Simply place a hot cooked potato (or any root vegetable, really) inside, with skin intact. Give it a gentle squeeze and voilà! It extracts the insides and leaves the skin inside the ricing chamber, which you then pull out and compost or throw down the disposal. Ricers are also great for making spaetzle.

Silpat mats: Silpats prevent foods from sticking when baking. I resisted buying these for years, and then I found some discounted at Marshalls. After one use, I knew they were worth the money, and then some.

I have three: two small ones and one large one that's imprinted with a ruler and several circular guides—helpful when making pie crusts. I especially love using my large Pepto-Bismol pink Silpat when rolling out dough and making pasta. Cleanup is so much easier now than in my pre-Silpat life.

Mini food processor: You can actually buy these for five to ten dollars, and they are worth every penny if you don't feel like chopping an onion or a carrot. Since they're small, they don't hog precious cupboard space. To clean, simply pop the blade, cup, and lid in the dishwasher.

Stand mixer: If you bake at least twice a week, I'd say this is a must. Although I occasionally pull out my electric mixer, I constantly use my fire engine–red KitchenAid mixer for making cakes, cookies, and breads. Just turn it on your chosen speed, and you're free to roam the kitchen and do other things. You can also buy fun attachments, like a pasta maker. Plus, stand mixers look ultra-cool and are available in virtually every color of the rainbow. I love my KitchenAid, but many other great brands are available.

COOKING NOTES

- All salt is sea or kosher salt.
- All chocolate is dark chocolate, preferably at least 65 percent cocoa.
- All sugar is vegan sugar.
- Flour is half whole wheat, half spelt, unless otherwise specified.
- Earth Balance is the only vegan margarine I use.
- Colavita Fruttato is my preferred extra-virgin olive oil.
- Vegenaise is the only brand of vegan mayonnaise I use. Full fat, please.
- Better Than Bouillon Vegetable is my preferred brand of stock.

Added salt: Many of my recipes call for salt to taste. When following a recipe that uses stock, please keep in mind that if the stock contains added salt, you probably will not need to add any to the recipe.

Pressing tofu: Place a few paper towels on a large plate. Place tofu on towels and then top with a few more paper towels. Place another plate on top, and weigh down with two heavy books (dictionaries would do nicely.) Let sit for 30 minutes, then flip, replace paper towels, and let sit for 30 more minutes. Cut in half lengthwise, and then cut in half again. Repeat until you have about 16 to 20 pieces; they don't have to be perfectly equal. Set aside.

Steaming tempeh: Most of my recipes with tempeh require you to steam it first to remove its inherent bitterness. To do this, simply place chunks or steaks in a steamer and steam, covered, over boiling or almost-boiling water for about 10 minutes, give or take.

Canned beans: When using canned beans, I suggest you rinse them to wash away added sodium, and then drain them.

I always use 1 heaping tablespoon of soy flour plus 1 tablespoon of water or soy milk as a substitute. Ironically, I learned of this tip and began using it years ago, long before I was vegan, thanks to *The Tightwad Gazette* by Amy Daczyzyn. (And yes, giving up eggs is cost-effective in the short term, and probably in the long-term as well, if you add in the cholesterol/health benefit factor.) I also add about one-third more baking powder than an egg-centric recipe would call for, just for good luck.

I've listed other egg substitutes below, equal to one egg. Experiment and find the ones that work best for you.

- 1 heaping tablespoon soy flour plus 1 tablespoon water: My old standby.
- ½ mashed banana: Obviously, only use this in sweet baked goods. It won't exactly make the tastiest quiche.
- 3–4 tablespoons applesauce: Again, only use this substitute in sweet baked goods.
- ¼ cup soft, pureed tofu: For best results, whiz in blender before adding to your batter.
- 3 tablespoons flaxseeds plus 2 tablespoons water: Whiz around in the blender before using. This is my least favorite method; I don't like the flaxy taste in baked goods, but some people do. (But they do provide important omega-3 fatty acids.)
- Store-bought egg replacer: Follow package instructions. (You can find it in most health food stores.)

MILK

The only problem with replacing dairy milk with non-dairy milk is deciding which kind you want to use. Soy, rice, hemp, coconut, oat, and almond milks occupy several shelves and half the so-called dairy aisles in my local Whole Foods market—and even in most mega box–shop markets I visit. You'll find vegan half-and-half, vegan creamers, vegan whipped creams, and vegan yogurts, sour creams, and puddings. No problemo here.

BUTTER

Margarines are processed foods, so you shouldn't indulge in them every day. They are for special occasions and holidays only! Earth Balance is the best vegan margarine I've found; I never use anything else.* If you are using another margarine, be sure it is made from nonhydrogenated oils.

My other favorite butter substitute is a mashed avocado, but I wouldn't use it for baking. Try it on toast. Sublime! You can also substitute oils for butter in most dishes.

HONEY

Agave nectar is a fabulous honey stand-in. Plus, it has a lower glycemic index, so it gives you a more even shot of energy; you won't crash and burn after eating it. Maple syrup, brown rice syrup, and corn syrup also work well. Stevia, an all-natural sweetener with zero calories and a low glycemic index, also works in certain dishes.

---

* **There has been some controversy about whether Earth Balance has been environmentally responsible in terms of purchasing the palm oil used in their product. According to the Earth Balance website, "Starting in 2011, Earth Balance will purchase Green Palm Certificates to fund the growth and expansion of sustainable palm." It seems that complaints have moved the company to act. So if something doesn't sit right with you, speak up. As Goethe said, "The world only goes forward because of those who oppose it."**

THE ICONS

 Fast
Cooks of average experience can generally pull together these recipes in less than 30 minutes.

 Frugal
These recipes won't bust your budget since they are built on a foundation of cheap-and-cheerful pantry staples.

 Kid-Friendly
These foods tend to appeal to little fingers and still-developing palates.

 Make Ahead
These recipes can be made a day or two in advance.

 Omnivore Friendly
Choose these recipes when trying to impress an omnivore. Generally speaking, they resemble the taste and texture of traditional non-vegan recipes.

NEW YEAR CELEBRATIONS

The New Year marks the first day of a brand-new calendar year. Different celebrations and rituals take place across countries and cultures, depending on which calendar you happen to follow.

Regardless of where you ring in the New Year, most people celebrate because it symbolizes a fresh start—a rebirth, if you will. We forgive ourselves for any mistakes we made during the previous year, we try to erase memories of our misfortunes, and then we make resolutions for improvement.

Many of my friends get sentimental on New Year's Eve, but I like the idea of plowing forward with abandon and a renewed sense of optimism, hope, and innocence. After all, what's past is past. There is only the present. And how you spend time right now can and will affect your future.

NEW YEAR'S DAY

The New Year is synonymous with fresh starts. This holiday always manages to wipe the slate clean, invoking feelings of innocence and rebirth, hence the endless resolutions. Not surprisingly, traditional New Year's foods center on good luck. And we certainly need the fortification, in order to keep all those resolutions!

MENU: GOOD LUCK BRUNCH

LUCKY SOBA NOODLES WITH DIPPING SAUCE

1 14-ounce package (approximately) soba noodles, cooked according to package directions and drained

Dipping Sauce
3 tablespoons soy sauce
2 cups vegetable, mushroom, or miso broth

Toppings
Mix and match any of the following:
1 sheet nori, snipped into tiny shreds with kitchen scissors
Sesame seeds or gomasio
Shredded carrots
Julienned cucumber
Dry-Fried Tofu cubes (see page 82)
Seitan or pre-steamed tempeh
Mung bean sprouts
Cooked, sliced mushrooms
Finely shredded cabbage
Finely shredded spinach
Cooked, shelled edamame

On New Year's Day, the Japanese eat long noodles to ensure a long life. The only catch is that you need to eat the entire noodle without breaking it. That said, slurping helps and is, in fact, encouraged. Kids especially love this dish because they can add whatever toppings they like (and they're allowed to slurp).

This recipe is a breeze to throw together—very helpful if you are hungover from ringing in the New Year the night before. The Japanese usually eat seasonally, and since the New Year appears in winter in the Northern Hemisphere, you should eat these noodles warm. When the hot summer months arrive, simply chill the noodles by running them under very cold water, and this dish will be a refreshing respite from the heat and humidity.

1. Divide well-drained noodles into four bowls.
2. Mix together soy sauce and broth to make the dipping sauce. (It should be served at room temperature.)
3. Top with just enough sauce to cover and allow diners to choose their favorite toppings.

Yield: 4 servings

HOT-AND-SOUR CARROTS AND LENTILS

In many countries, including Brazil, Italy, and Germany, it's considered good luck to eat legumes on New Year's Day. Think about it: Legumes like lentils, chickpeas, and peas are round—as in money, prosperity, and eternity. When the legumes swell, the hope is that your prosperity will follow suit. This dish combines North African and East Asian influences, marrying earthy cumin, hot cayenne, and tangy lemon, all contrasting nicely against a sweet-starchy carrot-lentil base. It's wonderful on its own on a cold January evening, or as a side. It's also tasty served over brown rice or the Golden Millet Pilaf (see page 125).

1. In a medium-size pot heat oil. Add onion, garlic, and cumin seeds and sauté until onion is soft, about 5 minutes. Add carrots and cook for another 10 minutes, stirring now and then.
2. Add spices and salt and stir to coat the veggies.
3. Add lentils, cinnamon stick, lemon, and broth. Bring to a boil, then lower heat to a hearty simmer. Cover and cook about 45 to 55 minutes, or until most of the water is absorbed. Stir in the herbs. Let cool 5 minutes before serving.

Yield: 6 servings

1 tablespoon olive oil
1 medium red onion, chopped
5 garlic cloves, sliced
1 teaspoon cumin seeds
2 cups peeled and diced carrots (diced to approximate lentil size)
1 tablespoon ground cumin
1 teaspoon cayenne pepper
½ teaspoon salt
1 cup brown lentils, rinsed and picked over
1 cinnamon stick
Juice of 1 lemon (about a scant ¼ cup)
2¾ cups vegetable broth
½ cup chopped fresh parsley
¼ cup chopped fresh cilantro

HOPPIN' JOHN

1 tablespoon olive oil

3 garlic cloves, chopped

1 red onion, chopped

1 organic green or red pepper, chopped

2 stalks organic celery, chopped

¼–½ teaspoon red pepper flakes

1 8-ounce package tempeh bacon, sliced or chopped

½ pound dried black-eyed peas, rinsed and soaked overnight or up to 12 hours

1 cup broccoli, chopped (frozen is fine)

1 cup chopped organic spinach (frozen is fine)

1 bay leaf

1 teaspoon salt

3 cups vegetable broth, plus up to 2 cups more

1 cup long-grain rice

Freshly ground pepper

Eating Hoppin' John for good luck on New Year's Day is traditional in the American South. New Year's Day is a landmark day for visiting friends and family. As the story goes, this dish gets its name from the welcoming phrase, "Hop in, John!" The contrast between the smoky tempeh bacon and creamy bean-rice mélange is sure to set the stage for a happy and healthy New Year. I added some extra greens to make this dish even healthier and more flavorful than it already is.

1. Preheat oven to 375°F.
2. Heat oil over medium heat in a large casserole. Sauté garlic, onion, green or red pepper, celery, and red pepper flakes until vegetables are soft, about 5 minutes.
3. Toss in the tempeh and sauté about 3 to 4 more minutes. The idea here is to infuse the oil with the tempeh's smokiness.
4. Add the drained black-eyed peas, broccoli, spinach, bay leaf, salt, and 3 cups broth. Bring to a boil, then lower heat to a simmer. Cook covered for 20 to 25 minutes, or until beans are tender.
5. Stir in rice. There should be approximately 2 cups of liquid left in the pot. You will have to rely on your judgment for this. Add more liquid as needed. Bring to a boil and, once again, cover and simmer for about 30 minutes, or until all water is absorbed.
6. Adjust seasonings. Drizzle with your favorite hot sauce and serve.

Yield: 8 servings

Wine Pairing

Aligoté, the "other white" from Burgundy, often has a slight smoky quality that will work beautifully with this dish.

CHINESE NEW YEAR

The Chinese Lunar New Year is a time to visit friends and family—and of course, to enjoy special foods. It's one of the most important Chinese holidays. Just before the New Year, everyone cleans their house from top to bottom to symbolically wipe clean any lingering bad luck from the previous year and to begin the New Year with a clean slate. On the same note, it's the time to get a new haircut or hairdo and wear new clothes. Traditionally, gifts of money are given in red envelopes to family members, and friends usually exchange small gifts of fruit or candy.

MENU: LUNAR NEW YEAR SUPPER

LEMON-CHAMPAGNE-BRAISED BABY BOK CHOY

Although baby bok choy is in the cabbage family, its taste is lighter and sweeter, which makes it perfect side-dish fodder. In this sweet-and-sour compilation, the lemon dances with the Champagne's fruit to add a hint of freshness. If Champagne is out of your price range, feel free to substitute Cava, a less expensive but equally wonderful Spanish sparkling wine. Oven-braising makes these baby boks a snap to prepare.

1. Preheat oven to 400°F.
2. In a shallow roasting pan, combine lemon juice, zest, Champagne, olive oil, soy sauce, garlic, nutritional yeast, agave nectar, and salt and pepper. Let sit for 10 to 15 minutes to allow garlic to infuse the marinade.
3. Place trimmed bok choy in marinade. Gently toss to ensure all leaves glisten with marinade. Cover with foil and oven-braise for up to 20 minutes or until bok choy is tender or tender-crisp, depending on your taste. (Check about halfway through cooking time to redistribute marinade and ensure that no leaves dry out.)
4. Drizzle with sesame oil, sprinkle with extra nutritional yeast, and serve.

Yield: 4 servings

Juice of ½ organic lemon
Zest of 1 organic lemon
¼ cup dry Champagne
1½ tablespoons olive oil
2 tablespoons soy sauce
1 garlic clove, minced
3 tablespoons nutritional yeast, plus extra for sprinkling
1 tablespoon agave nectar
Salt and pepper to taste
2 pounds baby bok choy, bottom stubs trimmed
Sesame oil for drizzling

Sauce

3 tablespoons Chinese fermented black beans (available at most Asian groceries), rinsed if you prefer less salt

1 cup vegetable broth

2–4 tablespoons soy sauce (depending on salt content of your broth)

2 tablespoons agave nectar

1½ tablespoons cornstarch

1 clove garlic, crushed

Tofu Mixture

1 pound extra-firm tofu, pressed (see page xi)

1 tablespoon peanut or canola oil

4 cloves garlic, crushed

1 large onion, chopped

1–2 tablespoons grated fresh ginger

¼–½ teaspoon crushed red pepper flakes or hot pepper oil

1 bunch broccoli, cut into bite-size florets

Thinly sliced scallions for garnish

TOFU WITH BROCCOLI AND BLACK BEAN SAUCE

This is one of my go-to quickie dinner dishes, yet it tastes special enough to serve as part of a holiday banquet.

1. To make the sauce, in a medium bowl whisk together the beans, broth, soy sauce, agave nectar, cornstarch, and 1 clove crushed garlic. Set aside.
2. To dry-fry the tofu, heat a wok or nonstick pan over medium heat. Gently pat the tofu pieces dry with a tea towel. Place the pieces on the dry wok, and cook, gently pressing down on the pieces now and then with a spatula. Flip when golden and repeat on the other side.
3. To stir-fry, heat oil in wok over medium-high heat, add garlic, onion, ginger, and hot pepper, stirring constantly, taking care not to let the garlic burn. The point here is to flavor the oil. Cook until onion is translucent. Add broccoli and stir-fry until it reaches your desired tenderness. (I like it tender-crisp.) Add tofu and continue to gently stir-fry. Top with sauce, stir gently, and serve over brown rice. Garnish with scallions, if desired.

Yield: 4 servings

Variations

Add any other "stir-fryable" veggies you like. I suggest shiitake mushrooms, thinly sliced organic red peppers, and/or snow peas. You can also replace the tofu with seitan.

MANDARIN ORANGE UPSIDE-DOWN CAKE

This is a fun twist on a classic American dessert recipe, and it presents so beautifully with the tiny Mandarin orange sections floating atop a caramel sea. The citrus notes are so light and refreshing against the syrupy topping and dense cake. Serve warm, perhaps with a scoop of vanilla soy ice cream.

1. Preheat oven to 350°F. Grease a 9-inch round cake pan.
2. In a small saucepan over medium heat, melt together ¼ cup Earth Balance, cinnamon, and all the brown sugar. Pour into greased cake pan and arrange well-drained oranges evenly on top.
3. In a large bowl, mix flour, granulated sugar, baking powder, and soy flour. In a medium bowl, mix milk, vanilla, orange-flower water, and the remaining ¼ cup Earth Balance, melted. Using a mixer, blend the wet ingredients into the dry ingredients and mix well.
4. Pour the cake batter over the Mandarin orange mixture and bake for about 45 minutes or until knife or cake tester inserted in center comes out clean. Remove cake from the oven and run a knife around the circumference of the pan to separate the cake from the pan's edge.
5. Allow cake to cool for at least 15 minutes—ideally 30 minutes. Place plate on top of cake pan, quickly invert, and remove pan.

Yield: 8 servings

½ cup Earth Balance, softened and divided
1 teaspoon cinnamon
¾ cup brown sugar
1½ cups flour
1 cup granulated sugar
1 tablespoon baking powder
1 tablespoon soy flour
1 cup soy milk
1 teaspoon vanilla
2 teaspoons orange-flower water (or substitute 2 teaspoons orange, lemon, or tangerine zest)
1 15-ounce can Mandarin oranges, drained well (this is very important if you don't want them to stick to the pan)

NOWRUZ
(PERSIAN NEW YEAR)

In Farsi Nowruz means "new day." This first-day-of-spring celebration marks the Persian New Year—and a symbolic fresh start. Families exchange presents after the exact moment of the equinox—and the celebration continues for an impressive thirteen days—my kind of holiday! Family members and close friends visit each other, exchange presents, and share food and love.

MENU: SPRING SWEETS

SEITAN WITH PRUNES

1 large onion, chopped
2 garlic cloves, crushed
1 tablespoon olive oil
¾ teaspoon turmeric
½ teaspoon cinnamon
1 pound seitan chunks, about
   1-inch cubes
2 cups vegetable broth
1 cup roughly chopped, pitted
   prunes
1 teaspoon lemon juice
2 tablespoons agave nectar or
   maple syrup

Face it: You're going to be eating a lot of sweets during Nowruz, so it's best to first line your stomach with something nutritious. This recipe is inspired by *khoreshe alu,* a Persian beef-based dish. I've replaced the meat with seitan, which happily drinks in the earthy, prune-based sauce. Serve this over rice or your favorite grain.

1. In a large casserole, heat oil over medium heat. Sauté onion and garlic until translucent, about 5 minutes. Add spices and sauté another minute or so, until everything is colored and fragrant.
2. Raise heat to medium-high and add seitan. Cook, stirring constantly, until seitan browns slightly.
3. Add remaining ingredients. Bring to a boil, then reduce heat. Cover and simmer till the flavors meld, about an hour.

Yield: 4 servings

BAKLAVA

I love baklava so much that I am considering changing my last name to Baclava. Close enough, right?

There are as many baklava recipes as there are cooks. After much trial and error, I've landed on this version, which uses a combination of meaty walnuts and pretty green pistachios. Feel free to play around with different combinations of spices and nuts. It's a very forgiving recipe—time-consuming but well worth the effort.

1. To make the syrup, boil water and mix in sugar and salt until dissolved. Remove from heat and stir in rose or orange-flower water.
2. Preheat oven to 350°F. Brush the bottom of a glass 9 x 13-inch pan with some of the melted Earth Balance.
3. In a large bowl, mix the walnuts, spices, and confectioners' sugar.
4. Place a sheet of phyllo pastry over the bottom and brush this with Earth Balance. Repeat 3 more times.
5. Spread the walnut mixture over the pastry. Gently press it down with your fingers.
6. Top with 3 or 4 more sheets of pastry/Earth Balance, as outlined in step 4.
7. Use a sharp knife and cut into serving-size diamonds, squares, or triangles.
8. Pour the rest of the melted Earth Balance over the pastry. Bake for 30 to 35 minutes or until crust is slightly crispy and golden. Remove from oven and pour the syrup over the pastry. Sprinkle with pistachios and let cool completely before serving.

Yield: About 24 pieces, depending on how large you cut them

Syrup

1 cup boiling water
1 cup sugar
Pinch of salt
¾–1 teaspoon rose or orange-flower water

Pastry

¾ cup (1½ sticks) Earth Balance, melted
4 cups ground walnuts (pulse gently in a food processor to grind)
2 teaspoons ground cardamom
½ teaspoon cinnamon
3 cups confectioners' sugar
1 16-ounce package vegan phyllo pastry, thawed
½ cup chopped pistachios

WORKING WITH PHYLLO

Working with phyllo sounds much more intimidating then it really is. The main thing you need to remember is that you must keep the delicate dough covered and damp so that it doesn't dry out.

To do this, lay a dampened tea towel on the counter. Spread the phyllo on the towel, and cover it with another damp tea towel or waxed paper, taking care to leave no phyllo exposed to the air. Remove one sheet at a time, and cover the remaining sheets with the towel in the interim.

FIGGY SPICED NUTS

1 cup walnuts
½ cup pecans
¼ cup cashews
¼ cup hazelnuts
¼ cup *pepitas* (pumpkin seeds)
½ teaspoon ground cinnamon
¼ teaspoon ground cumin
¼ teaspoon cayenne pepper
½ teaspoon salt
¼ cup light brown sugar
2 tablespoons Earth Balance
2 tablespoons water
½ cup de-stemmed and chopped
   dried figs or pitted and chopped
   dates

They're sweet. They're salty. They're spicy. These nuts offer something for everyone! Serve them along with plenty of strong, sweetened tea. Feel free to experiment with different types of nuts and play around with the proportions on the spices.

1. Toast nuts and *pepitas* in a dry skillet over medium-high heat, stirring often and taking care not to burn. Remove from heat immediately and transfer to a large bowl.
2. Mix spices, salt, and sugar in a small bowl and set aside.
3. Melt the Earth Balance in the same skillet in which you toasted the nuts. Add sugar-spice mixture and water. Gently stir in the nuts and figs and make sure everything is well coated. Remove from pan and spread evenly onto a foil-lined baking sheet or a Silpat mat.
4. Let cool and serve.

Yield: About 2 cups

MILK PUDDING (HALVAYE SHIR)

4 tablespoons Earth Balance
½ cup rice flour
1½ cups rice or soy milk
⅓ cup sugar
½ teaspoon ground cardamom
Pinch of cinnamon
Pinch of salt
1 tablespoon rose or orange-
   flower water
¼ cup pistachios, crushed

This delicate Persian pudding is the perfect thing to cleanse your palate after indulging in a hearty meal. I love the subtlety and lightness of the rose and orange-flower waters.

1. In a medium-size nonstick saucepan, melt Earth Balance over medium heat. Sprinkle in rice flour and stir continually until well combined, without letting the flour brown.
2. Whisk in the milk, stirring constantly. Reduce heat and continue cooking and whisking until thickened. Add sugar, spices, salt, and rose or orange-flower water. Cook about 5 more minutes.
3. Remove from heat. Divide among six ramekins and sprinkle with pistachios. Serve warm, cold, or at room temperature.

Yield: 4 servings

ROSH HASHANAH

The celebration of the New Year is one of the most important Jewish holidays. A time for reflection, practitioners review the mistakes they made during the previous year and vow to begin the New Year with a fresh start and better intentions. Of course, with the New Year come symbolic foods to enjoy with family.

MENU: NEW YEAR NOSH

EZ TZIMMES

The Yiddish word *tzimmes* comes from the German *zum essen,* or "to eat." The dish has eastern European roots—and plenty of root vegetables. There are as many tzimme recipes as there are cooks. So feel free to play around with the proportions. That's how new traditions are born, after all.

1. In a large pot over medium heat, melt the Earth Balance. Add the onion and sauté until soft, about 5 minutes.
2. Add remaining ingredients and bring to a boil. Reduce heat. Cover and simmer for about 30 minutes, or until veggies are all soft.

Yield: 8 servings as a side

3 tablespoons Earth Balance
1 red onion, minced
4 carrots, sliced
2 parsnips, sliced
3 large sweet potatoes, peeled and diced
1 apple, peeled, cored, and diced
¼ cup diced dried apricots
¼ cup diced prunes
¼ cup raisins
⅓ cup agave nectar
Zest and juice of 1 orange
Juice of ½ lemon
1 cup water
½ teaspoon salt
½ teaspoon cinnamon
¼ teaspoon nutmeg
⅛ teaspoon allspice
¼ teaspoon pepper

FRUGAL KUGEL

1 cup vegan sour cream
1 cup vegan cream cheese, at
 room temperature
¼ cup plus 1 tablespoon Earth
 Balance, melted
½ cup plus 1 tablespoon sugar
1 teaspoon cinnamon, plus more
 for dusting
¼ teaspoon nutmeg
Pinch of salt
1 pound noodles, cooked, drained,
 and rinsed with cold water to
 stop the cooking process
½ cup raisins
1 tart apple, peeled and chopped
½ cup chopped dried apricots
1 cup slivered almonds

Kugels are mainstays of Jewish cuisine: filling, comforting, and crafted from pantry staples. This is my humble shiksa attempt at kugel, and I will be the first to say that no one's kugel is as good as your *bubby*'s. If *bubby* is vegan, try her recipe first. If she's not, then this kugel's for you.

1. Preheat oven to 350°F. Grease an 11 x 17-inch baking dish.
2. In a large bowl, beat together the sour cream, cream cheese, and ¼ cup Earth Balance. Add the ½ cup sugar, cinnamon, nutmeg, and salt and continue beating until smooth. Stir in the cooked noodles, raisins, apple, and apricots.
3. Pour into baking dish. Top with almonds, 1 tablespoon sugar, and a dusting of cinnamon. Pour the remaining 1 tablespoon melted Earth Balance over top so that a crust will form.
4. Bake for 40 to 50 minutes, or until set and the top is golden. Let cool for 10 minutes. Cut into squares and serve warm or at room temperature.

Yield: 8 servings

TEMPEH WITH CINNAMON AND APPLES

3 8-ounce packages tempeh,
 cubed and steamed (see page xi)
Salt and freshly ground pepper
 to taste
1 teaspoon ground cinnamon
1 large onion, peeled and cut into
 chunks
5 whole garlic cloves
1 bay leaf
1 cup veggie broth
1⅓ cups white wine
4 apples, cored and cut
 horizontally into 4 pieces
2 tablespoons agave nectar
Salt and pepper to taste

This is an interesting combination of sweet, savory, and earthy, plus it's a no-brainer to throw together—an important consideration when choosing holiday recipes. Serve this over a sweetish whole grain like wheat berries or spelt, or along with mashed potatoes, roasted yams, or squash and greens.

1. Preheat the oven to 375°F.
2. Place the tempeh, cinnamon, onion, garlic, and bay leaf in a roasting pan. Pour the broth and wine over everything and roast for 30 minutes, or until everything is soft.
3. Add the apples and agave nectar; toss everything gently. Roast for about 30 more minutes, or until the apples are very soft and the tempeh and onions are cooked. Adjust seasonings.

Yield: 6–8 servings

AGAVE CAKE (LEKACH)

Traditionally, sweets with honey are served on Rosh Hashanah to set the tone for a sweet New Year. But as we vegans know, there's more than one way to sweeten a cake. Agave nectar does the trick here, and as a special added bonus, it has a very low glycemic index. What does this mean? You will still crash and burn after indulging in this sweet treat, since the recipe contains cane sugar, but the crash won't be as severe as if you had used honey.

1. Preheat oven to 325°F. Grease and flour a 9 x 13-inch loaf pan.
2. In a large mixer bowl, beat agave nectar and sugar together. Add coffee, then add baking powder, baking soda, and Earth Balance.
3. Add flours, about a cup at a time, then beat in cinnamon, nutmeg, and salt. Beat until smooth.
4. Pour into prepared pan. Bake for 50 to 60 minutes or until a cake tester comes out clean.
5. Serve at room temperature.

Yield: 1 loaf, about 10 servings

1⅓ cups agave nectar
1½ cups sugar
1 cup strong, black coffee
1 tablespoon baking powder
1 teaspoon baking soda
4 tablespoons Earth Balance, softened
4 cups flour
¼ cup soy flour
1½ teaspoons cinnamon
¼ teaspoon nutmeg
¼ teaspoon salt

Variations

Add 1 cup of any of the following during step 3:
raisins, cranberries, chopped walnuts, or chopped pecans.

AMERICAN CELEBRATIONS

As any American will tell you, in the United States we celebrate so many holidays that sometimes, figuring out when the banks are open or if you need to check in at the office can be downright confounding. But America is a melting pot of cultures and traditions, and so are our holidays. We celebrate a variety of unique secular and religious feasts. They contribute to our national identity and also inspire some damn tasty menus.

MARTIN LUTHER KING DAY

In 1964, Dr. Martin Luther King Jr. became the youngest man to win the Nobel Peace Prize for his work to end racism through civil disobedience and nonviolence. Dr. King worked tirelessly to end poverty and oppose war. Even though he was assassinated in Memphis in 1968, the momentum of the seeds of change he had planted had only just begun. Dr. King was posthumously given the Presidential Medal of Freedom in 1977 and the Congressional Gold Medal in 2004. Today we remember this great man by taking the day off work to serve charities. Why not also extend this charity to our furry friends and enjoy a Southern-inspired meatless meal?

MENU: SOUL FOOD FIT FOR A KING

SWEET MINT TEA

Sipping on this smooth, refreshing tea immediately catapults you into the land of porch swings and Southern drawls. I've included both hot and cold versions so people in all climates and in all seasons can enjoy.

1. Add the tea to a teapot and pour in 1 cup of the boiling water. Cover and let steep 4 minutes.
2. Add the agave nectar and mint leaves and stems. Pour in the rest of the hot water. Cover and let steep for 10 more minutes, stirring once or twice. Strain the mint tea into heatproof glasses and finish with a sprig of mint.
3. To serve ice tea, chill the tea in the refrigerator overnight.

Yield: 4 servings

1 quart boiling water
1 tablespoon loose green or white tea, or 3 bags green or white tea
⅔ cup agave nectar
3 cups firmly packed mint leaves and tender stems, crushed, plus a few sprigs for garnish

THAI-CENTRIC CREAMY MAC

4 cups elbow macaroni, uncooked

1 organic red pepper, roughly chopped

1 sweet onion, roughly chopped

1 large carrot, roughly chopped

2 tablespoons coconut oil

¼ teaspoon red pepper flakes

1 cup hemp, soy, or rice milk (in order of preference)

¼ cup coconut creamer or coconut milk (light is fine)

1 cup nutritional yeast

¼ teaspoon sea salt, or to taste

Warning: This is not your grandma's mac and cheese, although it's every bit as comforting and decadent. This version is infused with extremely subtle Thai influences: Its creaminess comes thanks to smooth and silky coconut oil and coconut creamer. (Don't worry! It's much more figure friendly than traditional mac and cheese.) A sprinkle of red pepper flakes infuses the sauce with an assertive bit of heat, which balances beautifully against the sweetness. You can use any brand of regular or whole grain elbow macaroni, but I prefer Barilla; each piece has little ridges to help the sauce stick to the pasta.

1. Cook macaroni according to package directions, but make sure it is staunchly al dente. It should remain slightly chewy. Drain.

2. Meanwhile, in a food processor whiz together red pepper, sweet onion, and carrot until it almost forms a paste.

3. In a large saucepan or stockpot, heat coconut oil over medium-low heat. Toss in red pepper flakes and cook for 1 minute or so to infuse the oil. Toss in the veggie paste and cook until fragrant and soft, about 7 minutes.

4. Stir in the milk and the coconut creamer, then whisk in the nutritional yeast. Bring to a boil, lower to a simmer, and cook until it thickens slightly. (If you prefer a thicker sauce, simmer slightly longer. If you prefer a thinner sauce, reduce simmer time.)

5. Add drained pasta to the sauce. Toss to coat and add salt.

Yield: 8 servings; recipe is easily doubled or tripled

Variations

Add 2 cups of any of the following during step 5: steamed broccoli or cauliflower, peas, corn, edamame, or chopped organic spinach.

DIRTY RICE

Foods that are built on simple ingredients usually taste the best, and Dirty Rice is no exception. This is classic Southern fare at its best. I could eat the whole pot.

1. Heat oil over medium heat in a large saucepan. Sauté mushrooms, onion, garlic, celery, and red pepper until soft. Sprinkle with salt.
2. Add rice and stir to coat with oil. Add remaining ingredients and bring to a boil. Reduce heat to low, cover, and simmer for about 40 minutes, or until all the liquid is absorbed. Adjust seasonings and serve.

Yield: 8 servings

2 tablespoons olive oil
8 ounces mushrooms, finely chopped
1 onion, finely chopped
5 cloves garlic, minced
1 stalk celery, finely chopped
1 red pepper, seeded and finely chopped
¼ teaspoon salt
2 cups uncooked brown rice
4 cups vegetable broth
3 tablespoons tomato paste
½ teaspoon ground black pepper
½ teaspoon cayenne pepper
1 cup thinly sliced green onions

Variation

To make this an entree, add a can of chickpeas or your favorite beans (drained and rinsed). Black-eyed peas are my favorite for this entree.

LEMON-CORNMEAL DIAMONDS

A whisper of lemon zest adds an element of lightness to these hearty cookies. Reminiscent of shortbread, they're wonderful for breakfast, dipped in coffee or tea, or as a fuss-free dessert.

1. Preheat oven to 325°F. Line two large baking sheets with Silpats or parchment paper.
2. Sift dry ingredients together in a large bowl.
3. In another large bowl, cream sugar and Earth Balance. Beat in the dry ingredients, about 1 cup at a time, stirring well between additions and scraping down the sides of the bowl. Add lemon zest and juice, and enough milk to form a smooth dough.
4. Place dough on a Silpat or floured surface and knead until smooth. Roll into a 1-inch-thick rectangle. Cut into diamond shapes, measuring about 2 inches at their widest (or whatever shapes you want. Who am I to stifle your creativity?).
5. Place on cookie sheets, spacing them about 2 inches apart. Bake until golden, about 30 minutes. Cool on a rack.

Yield: About 40 cookies

2 cups whole wheat pastry flour
1¼ cups yellow cornmeal
¼ cup soy flour
¼ teaspoon turmeric (for color)
Pinch of salt
¾ cup sugar
1 cup (2 sticks) Earth Balance, softened
2 tablespoons finely grated lemon zest
1 tablespoon lemon juice
Up to ¾ cup soy, rice, or coconut milk

MOTHER'S DAY

Moms work selflessly all year without any expectations. Mother's Day is a time to fete moms and thank them for all their love, affection, and attention. Surprise her with a special breakfast in bed. The kids can help with several of these recipes.

MENU: BREAKFAST IN BED FOR MOM

1¾ cups flour
2 heaping tablespoons soy flour
¼ teaspoon salt
1½ teaspoons poppy seeds
¾ cup sugar
2 teaspoons baking powder
¾ cup soy or rice milk
½ cup canola oil
1½ teaspoons lemon extract
Juice of ½ lemon
Zest of 1 lemon

LEMON POPPY-SEED MUFFINS

Featherlight and bright as sunshine, these polka-dotted, citrusy muffins are a classic for a reason. Mom will love one or two, slightly warmed and smeared with her favorite jam, along with tea in the prettiest cup you can find.

1. Preheat oven to 375°F. Spray muffin tins with cooking spray or insert paper baking liners.
2. Mix all dry ingredients in a large bowl.
3. Mix wet ingredients, including lemon zest, in a medium bowl. Stir into dry ingredients until just moistened. Do not overmix. This will result in tough muffins.
4. Bake for 15 to 20 minutes or until top is slightly golden.
5. Cool on a rack for about 10 to 15 minutes before serving.

Yield: 12 muffins

GRAPEFRUIT BRÛLÉE

Sure, you can bring your mom/spouse/partner a grapefruit half in bed, sprinkle it with sugar, and she will love you for it. But if you really want to impress her, this recipe increases the "wow" factor by about 200 percent. Plus, any recipe with a French name automatically gets extra brownie points.

1. Preheat the broiler.
2. Place grapefruit halves on a cookie sheet. If using alcohol, sprinkle it over the halves, then sprinkle liberally with sugar. Dust with cinnamon, if desired.
3. Place grapefruit halves about 4 inches under the broiler and broil for about 4 to 5 minutes, or until sugar caramelizes. Serve warm.

Yield: 1 or 2 servings

1 pink grapefruit, cut in half and pre-sectioned

A splash of her favorite fruit-compatible liquors (optional, but yummy; try Cointreau, Grand Marnier, rum, or brandy)

About 3 tablespoons Demerara or brown sugar (you can use white sugar, but Demerara or brown "burns" and tastes better)

Dusting of cinnamon (optional)

Variation
Use an orange or lemon instead. If using lemon, consider upping the amount of sugar.

DECONSTRUCTED STICKY TOFFEE–BANANA SMOOTHIE

This is like a liquid version of the famously decadent English dessert with the added creaminess of a ripe banana. Once Mom tastes this, she'll ask you to make it for her again and again. This includes one serving for Mom and one as a reward for you.

Process everything in a blender until smooth. Add more ice, if needed.

Yield: 2 servings

2 cups almond milk

1 cup pitted Medjool dates (the softer, the better; please only use Medjool dates)

½ teaspoon vanilla extract

Scrapings from 1 vanilla pod

2 very ripe bananas, frozen

1 cup ice cubes

Variation
Add some rum, if you want a little kick.

MEMORIAL DAY

You can wear white whenever you please, but summer produce and swimsuit weather comes just once a year. This menu celebrates summer's arrival with colorful, festive foods that welcome the warmth.

MENU: SUMMER KICK-OFF PICNIC

CAPRESE SANDWICH

4 tablespoons extra-virgin olive
  oil, plus extra for drizzling
2 tablespoons soy sauce
Lots of freshly ground pepper
  and salt
1 pound extra-firm organic tofu,
  cut into 4 equal slabs
1 loaf ciabatta bread, cut into
  4 pieces, and then cut in half
  horizontally (or use 4 ciabatta
  rolls)
1–2 large tomatoes, sliced
About ⅓ cup whole, fresh basil
  leaves

The original Caprese Sandwich is a classic, made from just five basic ingredients: crusty bread, good-quality olive oil, basil, cheese, and tomatoes. When you think about it, fresh mozzarella cheese itself is bland, requiring a drizzle of olive oil and a healthy sprinkle of salt and pepper to bring it to life. Just like mozzarella, tofu is also bland, moist, and undergoes a magical flavor transformation with the help of a few summertime staples. These sandwiches travel well and make great picnic treats. Just wrap them in aluminum foil and go! As with all recipes, the trick to an excellent Caprese Sandwich is using only the best-quality ingredients.

1. To prepare the marinade, mix oil, soy sauce, and freshly ground pepper in a shallow pan. Soak the tofu in the marinade for at least an hour (preferably overnight), turning occasionally to ensure all sides soak up the marinade.
2. To make the sandwiches, drizzle each bread slice with about 1 teaspoon olive oil. Layer the bread with 1 slice of tofu, 1 or 2 slices of tomato, and basil to taste. Season with salt and pepper, and if you're in a hedonistic mood, add another drizzle of extra-virgin olive oil. Press together slightly and enjoy!

Yield: 4 servings

GREEN LENTIL AND SMOKY TEMPEH SALAD

Smoky tempeh bacon is a nice contrast to the starchy-sweet lentils and slightly puckery dressing. Plus, since it's portable, this salad is perfect picnic fare.

1. Heat 2 tablespoons oil in a large stockpot over medium heat. Cook the garlic and onion until soft, taking care not to burn the garlic, about 5 minutes. Add the tempeh bacon and sauté for about 5 more minutes, to flavor the oil.
2. Add the broth, lentils, and bay leaf. Bring to a boil, then reduce heat, cover, and simmer until lentils are soft and all the water is absorbed, about 30 to 45 minutes. Drain and set aside.
3. In a small bowl, whisk together the remaining 6 tablespoons oil, vinegar, and Dijon mustard. Toss with the remaining ingredients in a large salad bowl and season with salt and pepper. Serve warm or at room temperature.

Yield: 12 servings as a side

2 tablespoons plus 6 tablespoons extra-virgin olive oil
3 garlic cloves, finely chopped
1 onion, chopped
1 8-ounce package tempeh bacon, sliced thinly
6 cups vegetable broth
1 pound French green lentils, rinsed and picked over
1 bay leaf
¼ cup balsamic or red wine vinegar
2½ tablespoons Dijon mustard
½ cup parsley
½ cup chopped red onion
½ cup shredded carrots
½ cup walnuts, toasted
Salt and pepper to taste

Variation

Substitute any small dried beans (e.g., adzuki, small white beans) for the green lentils.

Wine Pairing

Red wines from France's southwestern province of Gascony, where lentils are a staple, are typically earthy and hearty—and a great match for this dish.

EAT LIKE AN EGYPTIAN

Think lentils are important to contemporary vegans? Archaeologists have found lentils in Egyptian tombs dating as far back as 2400 BC.

MARINATED MIXED MUSHROOMS

6 tablespoons olive oil

5 garlic cloves, minced

2 pounds mixed mushrooms, chopped (I like a blend of baby bellas or cremini, shiitake, and oyster mushrooms)

½ cup chopped Italian parsley

½ cup dry white wine (like a Pinot Grigio)

1½ tablespoons red wine vinegar

1 teaspoon dried thyme

1 bay leaf

Salt and pepper to taste

Using a mix of mushrooms adds a little dimension to this classic picnic salad. I love these mushrooms with thick slices of crusty bread.

1. Heat oil in a large sauté pan over medium heat. Add garlic and sauté until soft, about 3 minutes. Strain out the garlic and set aside so it does not burn in the next step.
2. Add the mushrooms and parsley, raise heat to medium-high, and sauté until mushrooms are soft, about 10 minutes.
3. Stir in remaining ingredients and the reserved garlic and reduce heat to low. Simmer for about 5 minutes or until alcohol taste burns off, then cover and simmer 5 more minutes.
4. Cool, transfer to a container, and chill until cold. Drain before serving. Serve at room temperature.

Yield: 8 servings

Wine Pairing

Look for a lighter-bodied red with a hint of earthiness,
such as a Dolcetto from the mushroom-crazy Piedmont region of Italy.

RHUBARB-APPLE PIE

Rhubarb makes only a fleeting appearance in the markets. Fortunately, for many Americans, this also coincides with Memorial Day weekend. Spying the cheerful magenta stalks in the produce aisle is a sure sign that the warm weather has firmly taken hold. But most people still have a produce bin filled with winter's last apples. This pie seamlessly showcases the flavors of both seasons.

1. Preheat oven to 375°F.
2. In a large bowl, mix sugar, flour, baking soda, and spices. Add rhubarb, apples, and lemon juice and combine well. Set aside.
3. In another large bowl, mix flour and salt together. Cut in Earth Balance and shortening with a pastry blender until pea-size pieces appear. Sprinkle with 1 tablespoon of cold water, and use a fork to mix it in. Continue this process, adding a tablespoon of cold water at a time, until the dough begins to stick together. Remember: The less water you use and the less you mix, the flakier your crust will turn out.
4. Use your hands to form the dough into two balls. Place one ball on the center of a lightly floured surface or Silpat. (I love my large Silpat, not only because it makes cleanup a breeze, but also because it has measured templates for just about every pie size.) Roll out to a circle that's about an inch or two larger than your pie plate. Wrap it around the rolling pin and ease it onto the pie plate.
5. Roll out the other half of the crust as described above but set it aside.
6. Pour the filling into the pastry-lined pie crust. Gently top with the second crust. Trim the edges and crimp as desired. Cut a few air vents into the top to allow steam to escape. You can use mini cookie cutters, or, if you have Martha Stewart tendencies, you can also use your knife to cut stars, swirls, leaves, or the Mona Lisa into the crust.
7. If desired, gently brush the top of the pie with soy milk and sprinkle with coarse sugar.
8. Cover pie edges lightly with foil to prevent overbrowning. Bake for 20 minutes, then remove the foil, and bake for 25 to 30 more minutes or until top of pie is golden brown. Allow to cool completely on a wire rack before digging in.

Yield: 8 servings

Filling
¾ cup sugar
¼ cup flour
¼ teaspoon baking soda
¼ teaspoon cinnamon
¼ teaspoon ground ginger
4 cups chopped rhubarb, cut into ½-inch pieces
2 large apples, peeled and chopped into ½-inch pieces
¼ teaspoon lemon juice

Double Crust
2¼ cups flour
½ teaspoon salt
6 tablespoons Earth Balance, softened
4 tablespoons vegetable-based nonhydrogenated shortening
8–11 tablespoons cold water
2 tablespoons soy milk (optional)
1 teaspoon coarse sugar crystals (optional)

ORANGE DROP

2 organic oranges, peeled and cut into eighths

4 tablespoons vodka (orange flavored, if you have it)

6 tablespoons arancello (cousin to Limoncello but made with oranges instead of lemons)

2 tablespoons agave nectar

6 ice cubes

Fresh raspberries or sliced strawberries for garnish

This tangy twist on the more traditional Lemon Drop is bright, sunny, and the perfect summer kick-off drink.

1. Divide the oranges between two large glasses.
2. Process remaining ingredients in a blender until slushy and smooth and pour over the oranges. Top off with a berry—or three—and enjoy.

Yield: 2 servings

FATHER'S DAY

Dads do so much for us and get so little thanks. Take this opportunity to celebrate your papa with his favorite grilled foods, fresh summer produce, and sweet treats.

MENU: CHILL AND GRILL WITH DAD

CAPONATA

Caponata is a very manly dish, perfect for Father's Day. Back in the day, sailors who were going away for long periods of time always packed a supply of Caponata for sustenance. The vinegar prevented the veggie relish from going bad too quickly, and the vitamin C kept scurvy at bay.

You can serve Caponata as a side dish served with crusty bread, over brown rice or quinoa, or even tossed with pasta. This tastes best if you let it sit overnight and allow the flavors to meld before serving.

1 large eggplant
Salt
4 tablespoons olive oil
1 large sweet onion, finely chopped
3 celery stalks, chopped
5 garlic cloves, minced
1 red pepper, seeded and finely chopped
2 tablespoons capers, rinsed
4 tablespoons raisins
½ cup chopped green olives (you can use the kind with pimentos)
¼ cup unsweetened applesauce
3 ripe tomatoes, chopped
6 tablespoons white vinegar
1 tablespoon sugar or agave nectar
2 tablespoons dried parsley
Salt and pepper to taste

1. Cut the eggplant into ¼-inch slices, sprinkle generously with salt, and let sit in a colander for at least 30 minutes. Rinse off the bitter bile, pat dry, and then dice into ¼-inch pieces.
2. In a large, high-sided pot, heat oil over medium heat. Add onion, celery, and garlic and sauté until translucent. Add pepper and cook for 5 more minutes, then add capers, raisins, olives, and applesauce. Sauté for 5 minutes, then add the remaining ingredients.
3. Bring to a boil, turn heat down to low—just above a simmer—cover, and cook for about 45 minutes or until all veggies are soft, stirring occasionally. Remove lid and cook for up to 15 more minutes to cook off any excess liquid.

Yield: 8 servings

GRILLED VEGGIES, ROMAN STYLE

Marinade

⅓ cup balsamic vinegar

⅓ cup extra-virgin olive oil

4 cloves garlic, minced

½ cup coarsely chopped basil
leaves

Salt and freshly ground pepper
to taste

Veggies

2 summer squash, cut lengthwise
into ½-inch slices

2 zucchini, cut lengthwise into
½-inch slices

1 tablespoon kosher salt

3 large ripe tomatoes, cut into
2-inch-thick slices

1 yellow bell pepper, seeded and
halved

1 red bell pepper, seeded and
halved

1 medium red onion, peeled and
sliced into ½-inch-thick rounds

1 bunch asparagus, trimmed

2 small eggplants, cut lengthwise
into ½-inch slices

3 portobello mushrooms, caps
and gills removed

Walk down practically any street in Rome, and you will encounter a shop window featuring artfully arranged grilled vegetables. If you want to achieve those famous grill marks for Dad, I have one word for you: patience. Let the veggies sit on the grill for at least five minutes before peeking. And when it's time to check for grill marks, do it as gingerly as possible, taking care not to move the slices.

1. Combine all marinade ingredients in food processor. Whiz until smooth.
2. Place veggies in a large shallow dish (you may need two). Top with marinade and refrigerate 8 hours or overnight, turning once.
3. Grill the drained vegetables over hot coals until tender, about 5 to 10 minutes each side, depending on the vegetable.

Yield: 6 servings

Variations

Tofu and tempeh also love this marinade. Grill tofu for 6 to 8 minutes on each side. Steam the tempeh for 10 minutes before marinating; grill for 5 minutes on each side.

BLACK BEAN BURGERS

These are "manly man" burgers: substantive, a little tough, and yes, a little tender. You can grill them or bake them. They're wonderful served on a bun with the usual suspects: lettuce, onion, and tomato. I also like to add thinly sliced avocado to complement the Southwestern flavors.

1. In a large bowl, mash the beans with a fork or a potato masher.
2. Place pepper, onion, carrots, and garlic in a food processor and whiz until very finely minced. Stir into the bean mash, and add 1 tablespoon ketchup.
3. Add spices, cilantro, and bread crumbs and mix until the mixture sticks to itself. If mixture seems too dry, add 1 tablespoon ketchup at a time until sticky. Form into 4 patties.
4. If grilling, place the patties on oiled foil and grill for 10 minutes on each side. If baking, bake in a 350°F oven for about 10 to 12 minutes on each side.

Yield: 4 servings

1 15-ounce can black beans, rinsed and drained
½ red pepper, seeded and minced
½ small onion, minced
1 carrot, shredded
3 garlic cloves, minced
1 tablespoon ketchup, plus more as needed
1½ teaspoons cumin
½ teaspoon ground coriander
2 tablespoons chopped fresh cilantro
¾ cup bread crumbs
Salt to taste

Wine Pairing

A juicy, refreshing rosé from Provence will complement the spices.

Limoncello Cuppers

1 heaping tablespoon soy flour
1¼ cups unbleached all-purpose flour
1 teaspoon baking powder
¼ teaspoon baking soda
¼ teaspoon salt
1 tablespoon Limoncello
1 cup soy or rice milk
1 teaspoon vanilla
1 teaspoon lemon juice
1 tablespoon finely grated lemon zest (from about 2 lemons)
½ cup (1 stick) Earth Balance, softened
¾ cup sugar

Limoncello Icing

¼ cup vegan cream cheese, softened at room temperature for an hour
¼ cup (½ stick) Earth Balance, softened
2 tablespoons Limoncello
1 tablespoon finely grated lemon zest
1 teaspoon fresh lemon juice
2–2½ cups confectioners' sugar
Pinch of salt
¼–½ teaspoon turmeric for color (stale turmeric works best; see Nature's Food Coloring, page 29)

LIMONCELLO CUPCAKES

These pastel cuppers are as light as summer sunshine. The slight sourness of the lemon, liqueur, and zest balances the cloying sweetness of the icing.

They make a refreshing palate cleanser after all the Father's Day grilled goodies. This recipe is dedicated to Terry Hope Romero and Isa Chandra Moskowitz, the Queens of Vegan Cupcakes, to whom all vegan cupcake makers owe a debt—or at least a cupcake.

1. Preheat oven to 350°F. Line cupcake tins with liners or spray with cooking spray.
2. For the cuppers, mix together flours, baking powder, baking soda, and salt in a large bowl. Sift them first, if you have the time and inclination. (I usually don't!)
3. In another large bowl, mix together Limoncello, milk, vanilla, lemon juice, and zest.
4. Using your mixer, blend the Earth Balance and the sugar. Alternate adding some of the flour mixture, then some of the wet mixture. Continue mixing until smooth, scraping down the sides of the bowl occasionally.
5. Fill cupcake tins ⅔ full with batter. Bake for about 20 minutes or until a cake tester comes out clean.
6. Cool thoroughly on racks.
7. For the icing, use your mixer to combine the cream cheese and Earth Balance until well blended. Stir in the Limoncello, zest, and lemon juice. Add the turmeric and then confectioners' sugar, about ½ cup at a time till it's the consistency of most cream-cheese– or buttercream-style icings, scraping down the sides of the bowl as needed.
8. Lick the beaters. Ice the cupcakes. Decorate as desired.

Yield: 12 cupcakes

Nature's Food Coloring

These are more how-to instructions than recipes. The following proportions will color about ¼ cup of white icing. You'll need to double or triple the recipes and experiment with the intensities, depending on the quantities and types of food you want to color. Mix in the coloring well to avoid streaking.

Yellow: Add ¼ teaspoon and a large pinch of stale turmeric to the icing. Turmeric is often used to give vegan puddings and tofu scrambles that "eggy" shade. This is a good use for turmeric that's past its prime, since stale turmeric is fairly flavor neutral.

Blush: Using a sieve, mash the juice from 3 fresh or thawed frozen raspberries directly into the icing. Beet juice or beet root powder also works.

Mint green: With a fork, mash ¼ of a small avocado until creamy. Mix this into your icing. (The avocado makes your icing thinner, but in a fluffy, pleasant way.)

Raspberry: Using a sieve, mash the juice from 6 fresh or thawed frozen blueberries and 6 fresh or thawed frozen blackberries directly into the icing.

This list is certainly not definitive. Other natural sources of color include carrots (orange), annatto (yellow), beet juice (pink to red), and chlorella and spirulina (green). Experiment and color your world! And if you don't have time to make your own food colorings, please be safe and buy all-natural versions. They might not be as intense as the synthetic colors you're used to, but they are infinitely more healthful.

WHAT'S IN *YOUR* FOOD COLORING?

As anyone with kids can tell you, food coloring can bump up one's perception of taste—one reason why they're so widely used in the United States. But the neon colors of traditional food colors scare me—and with good reason. Many food colorings approved by the U.S. Food and Drug Administration are actually banned in other countries.

A few cases in point: A known carcinogen, FD&C Red No. 40 is banned in Denmark, Belgium, France, Germany, Switzerland, Sweden, Austria, and Norway. FD&C Yellow No. 5 is banned in Austria and Norway because it's linked to asthma attacks and thyroid tumors.

FOURTH OF JULY

Firecrackers. Swimming. Parades. It's fun to celebrate our nation's birthday. You can add even more significance to "independence day" by enjoying a tasty picnic meal that is independent of meat and cruelty.

MENU: INDEPENDENCE DAY PICNIC

OLD BAY CAKES

1 pound extra-firm tofu, drained and pressed for 2 hours (see page xi)

1 small onion, minced as finely as possible

¼ cup Vegenaise

⅓ cup bread crumbs

2 teaspoons Dijon mustard

1–2 tablespoons Old Bay Seasoning, or substitute Old Bay–Style Seasoning Mix (see page 31)

Dash of kelp powder (optional)

Salt and pepper to taste

½–1 cup flour for dredging

Oil for frying

4–6 lemon wedges

During summer across the East Coast, people dig into crab cakes. Crab cakes, made with Old Bay Seasoning, are a Baltimore tradition. (Old Bay Seasoning can be found either in the spice section or seafood—I know, I know—section of most large supermarkets or gourmet shops. But if you cannot find this seasoning, I've included a recipe on page 31 for making your own.)

I've always thought that boiling anything alive is exceptionally cruel, and I don't see why people can draw the line with crabs and mussels. Mixing tofu with this seasoning creates a patty that is virtually indistinguishable from crabs.

1. In a large bowl, using your fingers, squish the tofu until it resembles cottage cheese. Add onion, Vegenaise, bread crumbs, mustard, and seasonings. Mix well. Add more bread crumbs if the mixture is too wet and more mayonnaise if too dry.
2. Form into patties. Refrigerate for 1 hour.
3. Dredge each patty in flour.
4. Fry until golden brown, about 10 minutes on each side. Be gentle when flipping.
5. Serve with a lemon wedge.

Yield: 4–6 patties, recipe is easily doubled

OLD BAY–STYLE SEASONING MIX

This seasoning mix enhances the flavor of any seafood. You might find yourself using it in other foods as well.

Using a spice grinder, pulverize all ingredients into a fine powder. Keep leftovers tightly covered for about a year.

Yield: About ¼ cup

1 tablespoon ground bay leaves
2 teaspoons celery salt
1½ teaspoons dry mustard
1 teaspoon ground black pepper
½ teaspoon ground white pepper
⅛ teaspoon ground nutmeg
½ teaspoon ground cloves
¼ teaspoon ground allspice
½ teaspoon ground ginger
1 teaspoon paprika
¼ teaspoon crushed red pepper
flakes

BALSAMIC-BAKED BEANS

Baked beans are de rigueur for a summer picnic, but the sweet-sour addition of balsamic vinegar infuses these little bundles of fiber with a surprising elegance.

1. Preheat oven to 375°F.
2. In a large skillet, heat oil over medium heat. Sauté the tempeh bacon, onion, and garlic until the onion is soft, about 5 minutes.
3. Add remaining ingredients and mix until everything is well combined.
4. Transfer everything to a large, greased casserole and bake uncovered for 45 minutes to 1 hour, stirring occasionally.

Yield: 8–10 servings

2 tablespoons olive oil
1 cup diced tempeh bacon
1 medium onion, chopped
2 garlic cloves, minced
⅔ cup packed brown sugar
¼ cup tomato paste
4 tablespoons balsamic vinegar
1 tablespoon tamarind paste
1 tablespoon mustard
½ teaspoon pepper
½ teaspoon cayenne
1 tablespoon soy sauce
3 15-ounce cans of your favorite
beans, drained and rinsed

GOOD OLD-FASHIONED MACARONI SALAD

2 cups uncooked elbow macaroni

½ cup Vegenaise (do not use low fat)

2 tablespoons white vinegar

¼ cup sugar

1 tablespoon mustard

½ teaspoon salt, or to taste

¼ teaspoon freshly ground black pepper

Pinch of cayenne pepper

1 medium onion, finely chopped (using red onion makes a prettier salad)

1 celery stalk, finely chopped

1 green or red pepper, seeded and finely chopped

⅓ cup grated carrot

What would a summer picnic be without macaroni salad? This classic version combines the sweetness of sugar, carrots, and Vegenaise with the acidity of the vinegar. It's not exactly health food, but I say, moderation in all things including moderation. Be sure to let this salad rest in the refrigerator for at least a few hours before serving to allow all the flavors to meld.

1. Boil macaroni for about 8 minutes, then drain and rinse in cold water to stop the cooking. It needs to be slightly chewier than al dente since it will soften a bit as it rests with other ingredients. Do not overcook!

2. Meanwhile, mix the Vegenaise, vinegar, sugar, mustard, salt, and both peppers. Gently stir in the veggies and pasta.

3. Refrigerate overnight, if possible, before serving, or at least for a few hours.

Yield: 6 servings; recipe is easily doubled or tripled

BLUEBERRY PIE

Blueberries are in season and cheaper in July, and that's when everyone pulls out their grandma's blueberry pie recipe. (This recipe isn't actually my grandmother's, but still, I think she would approve.)

1. Preheat oven to 375°F.
2. In a large bowl, mix sugar, flour, cornstarch, baking soda, and cinnamon. Add berries. Set aside.
3. In another large bowl, mix flour and salt. Cut in Earth Balance and shortening with a pastry blender and blend until pea-size pieces appear. Sprinkle with 1 tablespoon of cold water, and use a fork to mix it in. Continue this process until the dough begins to stick together. Remember: The less water you use and the less you mix, the flakier your crust will turn out.
4. Use your hands to form the dough into two balls. Place one ball on the center of a lightly floured surface or Silpat (I love my large Silpat, not only because it makes cleanup a breeze, but also because it has measured templates for just about every pie size.) Roll out to a circle that's about an inch or two larger than your pie plate. Wrap it around the rolling pin and ease it into a 9-inch pie plate.
5. Roll out the other half of the crust as described above. Set aside.
6. Pour the filling into the pastry-lined pie crust. Gently top with the second crust. Trim the edges and crimp as desired. Cut a few air vents into the top to allow steam to escape.
7. If desired, gently brush the top of the pie with soy milk and sprinkle with coarse sugar.
8. Cover pie edges lightly with foil to prevent overbrowning. Bake for 20 minutes, then remove the foil, and bake for 25 to 30 more minutes or until top of pie is golden brown. Allow to cool completely on a wire rack before digging in.

Yield: 8 servings

Filling

¾ cup sugar
2 tablespoons flour
1 tablespoon cornstarch
½ teaspoon baking soda
¼ teaspoon cinnamon
3½ cups blueberries

Double Crust

2¼ cups flour
½ teaspoon salt
6 tablespoons (¾ stick) Earth Balance
4 tablespoons vegetable-based, nonhydrogenated shortening
8–11 tablespoons cold water
2 tablespoons soy milk (optional)
1 teaspoon coarse sugar crystals (optional)

MACEDONIA DI FRUTTA (ITALIAN FRUIT SALAD)

2 peaches, peeled and chopped
2 plums, peeled and chopped
1 apple, peeled, cored, and
  chopped
1 mango, peeled and chopped
½ pineapple, peeled and chopped
1 pint strawberries, hulled and
  halved
½ pint blueberries
½ pint raspberries
1 orange, peeled, seeded,
  sectioned, and cut into pieces
Juice of 1 lemon or orange
1–2 tablespoon agave nectar
Dash of cinnamon or nutmeg
Splash of Cava, Champagne,
  or Cointreau (optional but
  delicious)

A refreshing fruit salad is a must at any summer picnic. It's a light, healthy way to punctuate the meal and cleanse the palate—and to remind you to appreciate summer's bounty. This Italian-based recipe is extremely flexible. Use whatever is in season or is abundant.

Mix everything in a large glass bowl. Let sit overnight before serving to allow the flavors to meld.

Yield: 6–8 servings

LABOR DAY

We all work hard, and Labor Day is a time to banish all thoughts of toil, chill out, and enjoy good food and fun with family and friends. Given the spirit of the holiday, these recipes are fairly hands-off. Who wants to work on Labor Day, even in the kitchen?

MENU: LIGHT, LATE SUMMER PICNIC

LAZY BEAN DIP

This dip is a no-brainer to bring to picnics as is, with a colorful plate of crudités, or as a sandwich spread. Play around with different kinds of beans including chickpeas and lentils.

Mix everything in the food processor until the dip reaches your desired consistency.

Yield: About 1½ cups

1 15.5-ounce can cannellini beans, rinsed and drained
1–2 garlic cloves, sliced
1 tablespoon white vinegar
1 tablespoon lemon juice
3 tablespoons best-quality extra-virgin olive oil
¼ cup chopped fresh parsley
¼ teaspoon salt
Freshly ground pepper to taste
Water or vegetable broth (optional, add a little at a time if you prefer a thinner dip)

3 tablespoons white vinegar

2 tablespoons extra-virgin olive oil

4 tablespoons agave nectar

½ teaspoon vanilla

1 garlic clove, minced

1 teaspoon nigella seeds (if you can't find them, use caraway seeds)

Salt and pepper (preferably white pepper) to taste

4 cups shredded green cabbage (about ½ a small head)

2 cups shredded fennel (about 1 large bulb)

2 cups shredded radicchio

1 cup shredded carrots

6 green onions, thinly sliced

GENTRIFIED COLESLAW

Gentrification. It's happening everywhere: Things that fell out of favor are suddenly rediscovered and reinvented. It was bound to happen to coleslaw sooner or later, thanks to the addition of hipster veggies like radicchio and fennel. This slaw tastes best if you let it sit overnight; the vinegar will soften the veggies and allow the dressing to infuse them with a sweet-sour essence.

1. In a large bowl, whisk together the vinegar, oil, agave nectar, and vanilla. Add the garlic and nigella seeds, and season with salt and pepper.
2. Gently toss in the remaining ingredients. Cover and refrigerate overnight, or for at least 4 hours.

Yield: 8 servings as a side

BRAZILIAN PASTELS

Every culture has a dough-pocket recipe, and this one comes to us via Brazil. Since they are portable, they are no-brainers for picnics or for packed lunches for that matter. I like to eat them with a dollop of hot sauce.

1. Preheat oven to 400°F.
2. In a large bowl, mix flour and salt. With a pastry cutter, work in Earth Balance and shortening and process until roughly blended. Do not overmix or the dough will toughen. Add water, 1 tablespoon at a time, and use your hands to work it into a dough. The less water you use, the flakier your crust will be.
3. Roll out dough to a ¼-inch thickness. Cover with plastic wrap or waxed paper and refrigerate for 20 minutes.
4. While the dough chills, prepare the filling. In a small frying pan, heat the oil and sauté the onion until clear, about 5 minutes. Sprinkle with salt.
5. In a medium bowl, mix the crumbles with the onions and parsley. Using your hands is easiest.
6. Use a glass or cookie cutter to cut 10 3-inch circles from the dough. Flatten each out slightly and fill with about 1 tablespoon of filling. Do not overstuff! Fold over the dough and crimp the edges.
7. Place on a medium, greased baking sheet and bake about 9 to 15 minutes on each side or until golden. (Baking time will depend on how large you make your *pastels*.) *Bom apetite!*

Yield: 10–15 *pastels*, depending on size

Dough

1 cup flour

½ teaspoon salt

2 tablespoons Earth Balance

4 tablespoons nonhydrogenated vegan shortening

¼ cup cold water

Filling

½ tablespoon olive oil

½ medium onion, finely chopped

¼ teaspoon salt

7 ounces ground beef–style crumbles, or reconstituted TVP

2 tablespoons dried parsley

Variations

If you are inclined to decadence, you can fry the *pastels* in canola oil instead of baking them. Remove them when they are golden brown and drain them well on paper towels. You can also add vegan cheese, like Daiya, to the filling, or just use the cheese alone as the filling.

SANGRIA BLANCA

1¼ liter of dry white wine *

4 peaches, peeled and cut into
chunks

2 plums, peeled and cut into
chunks

1 orange or tangerine, peeled and
cut into chunks

About ¼ cup diced pineapple

Juice and zest of ½ organic lemon

8 strawberries, sliced

3 tablespoons sugar or agave
nectar

Frozen green grapes for garnish

* For an alcohol-free version,
substitute lemon-lime soda for
the wine and serve immediately.

This rejuvenating drink is perfect for Labor Day parties, since all of the fruit is in season, and it's easy to produce in mass quantities. And since it contains whole, fresh fruit, you could argue that it's healthy.

1. Mix everything in a pitcher. Chill well to allow the flavors to blend; overnight is ideal.
2. To serve, spoon some wine-soaked fruit into a clear glass along with 3 ice cubes. Top with sangria and a few frozen green grapes.

Yield: 1 pitcher, about 4–6 servings

COLUMBUS DAY

Columbus Day celebrates Columbus's arrival in the New World. (Yes, others got here first, and yes, they also deserve a national holiday.) Although this federal holiday was created in 1970 as a way to promote patriotism, many Italian-Americans also use this holiday to celebrate their heritage, culture, and of course, their cuisine, which—along with French and Chinese—is commonly considered to be one of the world's top three.

MENU: HOMAGE TO ITALY

PANZANELLA

This recipe is the epitome of frugality, relying on stale bread to add body and texture to basic salad greens. The ingredients and preparation are deceivingly simple, but then again, I think that the tastiest foods are often built upon the simplest ingredients. It makes a great first course, but I often eat this for dinner.

1. Slice the bread and soak it in vegetable broth. Squeeze out excess moisture (a good job for the kids!) and let it drain in a colander. When drained, separate the clumps so they look like small-but-wet croutons.
2. To make the dressing, pour olive oil into a small bowl. Whisk in the vinegar and agave nectar, then stir in the garlic, basil, and oregano.
3. Toss remaining salad ingredients in a large bowl. Gently stir in the "croutons," then finish with the dressing, and toss. Adjust seasonings and serve.

Yield: 4 servings

1 small loaf stale bread
4 cups vegetable broth
6 tablespoons extra-virgin
   olive oil
2 tablespoons balsamic vinegar
1 teaspoon agave nectar
2 garlic cloves, minced
¼ cup finely chopped fresh basil
2 teaspoons finely chopped fresh
   oregano
1 small head romaine lettuce
4 ripe tomatoes, seeded and
   chopped
1 English cucumber, peeled and
   thinly sliced
1 large red onion, thinly sliced
Salt and freshly ground pepper
   to taste

Variations
Add thinly sliced fennel, radicchio, endive, grated carrots,
or anything else that inspires you.

Wine Pairing
Most any Mediterranean rosé will sparkle alongside
basil, oregano, and tomatoes.

RISOTTO WITH LEEKS AND PORCINI MUSHROOMS

6 leeks, sliced thinly (you can use the dark green part, too)

2 cloves garlic, chopped

4 tablespoons olive oil

½ teaspoon salt

Fresh pepper to taste

6–8 cups vegetable stock

1 cup dried porcini mushrooms, crumbled

2 cups Arborio rice

2 tablespoons Earth Balance

Leeks infuse this risotto with a luxurious creaminess, and the porcini mushrooms add a subtle earthiness that complements the leeks' sweetness. You can substitute any dried mushroom you like, but porcinis really sing here.

1. In a large pan, sauté the leeks and garlic in olive oil over medium-low heat, until soft and fragrant, 20 to 30 minutes. Sprinkle with salt.
2. Meanwhile, in a large stockpot, heat stock to a simmer. Toss in porcini mushrooms.
3. When the leeks are soft, add the rice and stir to coat it with oil. Cook for 1 minute on medium heat.
4. Add broth, one ladle at a time. Allow rice to absorb broth and then repeat this process until rice is al dente—about 20 to 30 minutes.
5. Stir in Earth Balance, then close the lid and turn off the heat. After about a minute, mix again, adjust seasonings as needed, and serve.

Yield: 6–8 servings

SICILIAN-INSPIRED KALE

In this super-healthy side dish, slightly spicy, garlicky infused olive oil does a mad tarantella with kale and raisins. You can pimp this dish by adding chickpeas or white beans. You can also serve it over your favorite grain or tossed with a short pasta like orecchiette or rotini. I love to eat this with a fat slice of peasant-style bread, which I use to sop up the juices.

I large bunch kale, about 5–6 cups, chopped
1½ tablespoons olive oil
5 cloves garlic, crushed
½ teaspoon crushed red pepper
I cup vegetable broth
½ cup raisins
¼–½ cup toasted pine nuts
Salt and pepper to taste

1. Remove the stalks from the kale. Chop the remaining leaves as finely as you can; they should be in tiny shreds. Set aside.
2. In a large pot, heat oil over medium heat. Add garlic and red pepper, and gently cook until garlic is soft. Be careful not to burn; lower the heat if needed. If you're pressed for time, you can do this in about 5 minutes, but the longer the garlic can infuse the oil, the better this dish tastes. I try to stretch this step out to 15 minutes. (Adding salt to the garlic will draw out the oil and slow down the cooking process.)
3. Add the kale. Toss until covered with the oil mixture and cook for about 5 minutes.
4. Add the broth and raisins. Cover and cook for about 20 to 25 minutes, stirring occasionally. Add more broth, if needed. Remove from heat when kale is tender and most of the broth is absorbed. Top with toasted pine nuts and a drizzle of extra-virgin olive oil, if you're inclined to decadence.

Yield: 4 servings as a side

Wine Pairing

White wines from Sicily are hard to find in the United States, so for the perfect flavor match, look elsewhere on the Mediterranean—to the south of France to be specific. Whites from Provence are round, fleshy accompaniments to the bitter greens, sharp pepper, and sweet fruit.

KITCHEN WISDOM

When garlic or onions start to cook too quickly and are in danger of browning (my pet peeve), remove from heat and add salt. The salt draws out the water and slows down the cooking process. Return to heat when you have regained control of the situation.

ITALIAN MOJITO

10–20 fresh peppermint leaves, lightly chopped

½ teaspoon fresh lemon zest (use organic, if possible)

2 jiggers chilled Limoncello* (or to taste)

1 ¼ cups chilled sparkling water, plain or lemon flavored

* My first book, *The Urban Vegan,* includes a recipe for Homemade Limoncello.

Nothing is more cooling and summery than fresh mint paired with the puckery lemon flavor of Limoncello, a Sicilian digestivo. It's light, refreshing, and simple: perfect for hot weather imbibing.

Place the mint leaves and zest in a tall glass and muddle them with a pestle to tease out their flavors. Pour the Limoncello over the leaves, then top off with sparkling water. Adjust levels of water and/or liqueur to your taste.

Yield: 1 tall drink

CHOCOLATE-HAZELNUT POLENTA BUDINO

This *budino* (Italian for "pudding") is inspired by those chocolate-hazelnut spreads that I practically inhale anytime I'm in Europe. The corn-polenta base is inherently sweet and nicely offsets the bitterness of the chocolate and earthy candied nuts.

1. To make Candied Hazelnuts for the topping, follow the recipe for Candied Squash Seeds (see page 76) but substitute 1 cup chopped, skinned hazelnuts for the squash seeds and omit the herbs and cumin.
2. For the *budino,* in a medium saucepan, combine soy milk, sugar, vanilla, and salt. Bring to a simmer, then gradually whisk in ½ cup polenta. Cook for about 20 minutes on low, whisking and stirring often. It should thicken considerably and fairly quickly; don't be alarmed. Calmly add more soy milk, if needed.
3. For the Chocolate Sauce, melt all ingredients in a glass bowl in microwave at 50 percent power level. Start with 2 minutes, stir, and then nuke in 30-second intervals until the chocolate is melted and the sauce is glossy.
4. Divide the *budino* into individual bowls and top with a healthy glob of Chocolate Sauce and a handful of Candied Hazelnuts.

Yield: 4–6 servings

Pudding

1 cup chopped, skinned hazelnuts (rub the nuts with a tea towel to remove skins)

3¾ cups soy milk

½ cup sugar

1 teaspoon vanilla

½ teaspoon salt

½ cup polenta

Chocolate Sauce

½ cup best-quality dark chocolate (I recommend Valrhona if you can get it)

1 teaspoon vanilla

Pinch salt

About 2–3 tablespoons soy milk, or just enough to thin out the chocolate

Halloween

On Halloween you can become someone else for a day. Whether you dress up as an angel or a witch, you'll undoubtedly need a slew of creepy but tasty snacks to feed the mobs.

MENU: FRIGHTENINGLY GOOD GRUB

Witches' Fingers

1 cup (2 sticks) Earth Balance, softened

1 cup confectioners' sugar

1 teaspoon almond or rum extract

1 teaspoon vanilla

2⅔ cups flour

1 heaping tablespoon soy flour

1½ teaspoons baking powder

1 teaspoon salt

¾ cup whole, blanched almonds

Red food coloring (please get natural, if you can)

Rubber gloves (even natural food coloring stains!)

I made these "arthritic" little cookies one year for a Halloween party, not knowing how anyone would react to them. I assumed the littlest trick-or-treaters might be freaked out by the bloody fingernails and gnarly joints, but they gobbled up these cookies without question. They might look evil, but Witches' Fingers taste freakishly good.

1. In a large mixing bowl, beat together Earth Balance, sugar, extract, and vanilla. Add flours, baking powder, and salt, a bit at a time, mixing well and scraping down the sides of the bowl as needed.
2. Cover with a tea towel and refrigerate 30 minutes.
3. Divide the dough into four pieces.
4. Preheat oven to 325°F.
5. Put on your gloves. Remove ¼ of the dough from the fridge. Roll a 1-inch ball of dough into a finger-shaped cookie. Dip an almond into red food coloring, then press it firmly into the top end of the cookie end to make the nail. Using your finger, press down the center of cookie to make a "knuckle" shape. Use a small knife to make several slashes on the knuckle.
6. Place cookies on lightly greased or Silpat-lined cookie sheets; bake for 20 to 25 minutes or until just golden. Remove from cookie sheets and let cool on racks. Repeat with remaining dough.

Yield: About 5 dozen cookies

WORMY CIDER

What screams Halloween more than a punch bowl filled with cinnamony cider and oodles of squirmy worms? Make this drink about an hour before serving. You can buy vegan gummy worms online at www.naturalcandystore .com. Many natural foods stores, like Whole Foods, also carry them.

1 gallon apple cider
8 cinnamon sticks
4 whole cloves
½ cup packed brown sugar
3 cups orange juice
½ teaspoon cinnamon
2 cups vegan gummy worms (I recommend Surf Sweets brand)

1. Mix everything except the gummy worms in a large pot. Bring to a boil and then reduce to low. Simmer uncovered for about 20 minutes, stirring occasionally.
2. Let cool to room temperature. Remove cinnamon sticks and cloves, and pour into a punch bowl. Add the gummy worms and any other large decorations that might enhance the all-important "ew" effect. Think plastic brains, hands, and extra-large large spiders. (To avoid choking incidents, do not add anything bite-size or small that is inedible. And always remove the gummies before serving to small children.)

Yield: About 16 servings

STUFFED "ROACHES"

Doesn't sound vegan, does it? But these dark little treats have passed the vegan test with flying colors. They are the perfect way to both gross out and then delight trick-or-treaters of all ages. Don't forget to make a label to get the most nauseating effect possible.

½ cup vegan cream cheese, at room temperature
4 tablespoons confectioners' sugar
¼ teaspoon salt
1 teaspoon vanilla
30 large Medjool dates, pitted

1. In a medium bowl, combine cream cheese, confectioners' sugar, salt, and vanilla. Mix well.
2. Carefully fill each date with about 1 teaspoon of the cream cheese mixture and pinch it closed.

Yield: 30 treats

THANKSGIVING

Thanksgiving is a uniquely American holiday. It's a time to step back and express gratitude for all that we have: our family, friends, health, and homes. No matter how bad things get, most people concede that they have a lot to be thankful for. Many vegans and vegetarians, myself included, will tell you that they love this holiday because so many Thanksgiving foods are inherently animal-free. This herbivorous feast will provoke gratitude in your animal friends.

MENU: APPRECIATION CELEBRATION

SEITAN WITH QUINCE, APPLE, AND ONION

2 tablespoons olive oil
1 medium onion, sliced
2 cups seitan chunks (store-bought, use your own recipe, or use my recipe from my first cookbook, *The Urban Vegan*)
Salt and pepper to taste
2 small quinces, peeled and chopped into ½-inch dice
1 small apple, peeled and chopped into ½-inch dice
1 cup vegetable broth
½ teaspoon cumin
¼ teaspoon cinnamon
1 teaspoon ground sage
1 tablespoon brandy (optional)
1 tablespoon cornstarch

There's something elegant and comforting about this harvest combination with its warming, earthy herbs. This stewy dish makes its own gravy, perfect for serving with the Rutabaga-Fennel Clapshot (see page 47). You can also serve it alongside any grain or over noodles.

1. Heat oil over medium heat in a large casserole. Add onions. Sauté until soft, about 5 minutes.
2. Add seitan. Sauté, stirring constantly, about 10 minutes. Seitan should begin to brown a bit. Season with salt and pepper.
3. Add quince, apple, veggie broth, spices, and sage. Bring to a boil, then add brandy if desired. Cook for a minute or two to allow alcohol to steam off. Turn heat to low.
4. With a ladle, transfer about ¼ cup of broth to a separate bowl. Whisk in the cornstarch to make a smooth slurry, then stir it into the seitan mixture.
5. Cover and simmer for 20 minutes. Remove cover and cook for another 10 minutes. Adjust seasonings. Remove from heat and let sit for about 10 minutes before serving.

Yield: 4 servings; recipe is easily doubled

RUTABAGA-FENNEL CLAPSHOT

Clapshot potatoes are standard harvest fare—warming, comforting, and filling. The addition of rutabaga (or swede, as it's called in the United Kingdom), adds a hint of earthiness and depth, while sweet fennel seeds play against the rutabaga's bitterness, adding random explosions of licorice flavor.

1. Boil the rutabagas and potatoes in a large pot of salted water for about 20 to 25 minutes, or until soft.
2. Drain well and mash in a large bowl with fennel seeds, Earth Balance, oil, and milk. Adjust seasonings and serve.

Yield: Serves 8

1 large rutabaga, peeled and cut into 2-inch chunks

3 medium potatoes, peeled and cut into 2-inch chunks

1 tablespoon fennel seeds, soaked in hot water for about 5 minutes, then drained

3 tablespoons Earth Balance

1 tablespoon olive oil

¼ cup soy or nut milk

Salt and pepper to taste

LEFTOVER MAKEOVER

Form leftover Clapshot into patties or "nuggets," depending on your preference. Brown them in a large sauté pan in a bit of oil over medium heat and serve. You can transform the Colcannon (page 100) and Pimped Mashed Potatoes (page 50) using the same method.

KALE WITH RAISINS AND CHANA DAL (YELLOW SPLIT PEAS)

3 tablespoons olive oil
6 garlic cloves, sliced
4 tablespoons raisins or sultanas (golden raisins)
1 large bunch kale, large stems removed, finely trimmed to ½- to 1-inch strips
1 cup *chana dal* (yellow split peas)
1½–2½ cups vegetable stock
4 tablespoons dry white wine

The *chana dal* in this dish should be al dente and have a bit of bite to them. This teases out their nutty quality. Of course, if you prefer softer beans, then simply cook the mixture until the *chana dal* reaches the level of softness you prefer.

1. In a large stockpot, heat oil over medium heat. Add garlic and cook until it is soft, about 5 to 10 minutes. Be careful not to let it brown.
2. Add raisins and cook 1 minute. Add kale and *chana dal* and stir. Add stock and wine and bring the mixture to a boil.
3. Cover, turn heat to low, and simmer until kale is tender—about 50 minutes or so. Add more liquid as needed. Uncover. Turn heat to high and cook off the remaining liquid.
4. Serve warm or at room temperature.

Yield: 6 servings as a side dish

FIG-PECAN STUFFED ACORN SQUASH

2 acorn squash, halved lengthwise and seeded
1 tablespoon olive oil
Salt and pepper to taste
3 tablespoons Earth Balance, melted
⅓ cup agave nectar
¾ cup dried, de-stemmed, and chopped Calimyrna figs
⅓ cup chopped pecans
½ teaspoon cinnamon
¼ teaspoon nutmeg

This elegant dish looks as good as it tastes. The pecans and the mustiness of the figs contrast nicely against the inherent sweetness of the squash. The added shot of agave nectar intensifies the sweetness and elevates this to a special-occasion side status.

1. Preheat oven to 350°F.
2. Rub insides of acorn squash halves with olive oil and sprinkle with salt and pepper. Turn upside down and place on a foil-lined cookie sheet (for easy cleanup later). Bake for 30 to 40 minutes or until soft.
3. Meanwhile mix remaining ingredients together in a medium bowl
4. Remove squash from the oven and turn right side up. Fill halves with the fig mixture.
5. Bake for about 25 to 30 minutes or until filling is soft and bubbly.
6. Cool for about 10 minutes before cutting in half and serving.

Yield: 8 side servings

MUSHROOM-TARRAGON GRAVY

What would Thanksgiving be without gravy? The deep, earthy aromas of this mushroom-based gravy play nicely off the piquant licorice notes from the fresh tarragon. Serve it over stuffing, Pimped Mashed Potatoes (see page 50, but only use one of the more compatible versions), Rutabaga-Fennel Clapshot (see page 47), rice, or your favorite grilled seitan.

1. Heat oil over medium heat in a large frying pan. Sauté onion and garlic until soft, about 5 minutes. Add mushrooms, thyme, and freshly ground pepper. Sauté until mushrooms are soft, about 8 to 10 minutes.
2. Remove mushrooms from pan and set aside. Turn heat to high and pour in the wine. Deglaze the pan, scraping up any bits with a spatula. Add stock and return mushrooms to the pan. Bring to a boil and boil for about 15 minutes.
3. With a ladle, transfer about ½ cup broth from the pan into a medium bowl. Make a smooth slurry by whisking the cornstarch or arrowroot into this broth, followed by the sour cream.
4. Return the slurry to the frying pan and stir well so it's evenly incorporated. Cook until it reaches the desired consistency, about 5 to 10 minutes. Adjust seasonings. Stir in tarragon.

Yield: About 6 cups

2 tablespoons olive oil
1 small onion, finely chopped
4 garlic cloves, chopped
8 ounces shiitake mushrooms, chopped
8 ounces oyster mushrooms, chopped
8 ounces baby bella (cremini) mushrooms, chopped
½ teaspoon dried thyme
Freshly ground pepper to taste
¾ cup dry white wine
5 cups vegetable stock
2 tablespoons cornstarch or arrowroot
½ cup vegan sour cream
2 teaspoons chopped fresh tarragon

ADOPT-A-TURKEY

Each Thanksgiving, instead of eating a turkey, I adopt one from Farm Sanctuary. Since 1986, this program has saved turkeys from the dinner table and has raised awareness about the horrors of factory farming. Farm Sanctuary uses all its funds to rescue animals, care for them, and educate the public about and advocate for turkeys and other farm animals. When you adopt a turkey, you will receive a certificate, photos, and some interesting tidbits about your feathered adoptee. For more information, visit www .adoptaturkey.org.

About 1 pound potatoes (4 or 5 potatoes; the exact measure is not essential)

2–4 tablespoons softened Earth Balance

½ teaspoon salt, or to taste

Freshly ground pepper to taste

About ¼–⅓ cup rice or soy milk, for mashing

"Pimping" Ingredients

Pick 1 of the following:

1 tablespoon fresh ground ginger plus 2 crushed garlic cloves

2 tablespoons Vegenaise plus 1 cup chopped fresh herbs of your choice

4 tablespoons nutritional yeast, 2 tablespoons Dijon mustard, and 2 tablespoons agave nectar or maple syrup

Indian style mash: 1 teaspoon garam masala, ½ teaspoon cumin, and ¼ teaspoon turmeric

Japanese mash 1: 2 tablespoons miso, ½ cup sliced scallions, plus a drizzle of dark sesame oil

Japanese mash 2: 1 tablespoon wasabi paste plus a splash of good-quality soy sauce

Middle Eastern mash: ¼ cup tahini plus 1 tablespoon zaatar or sumac

Polish mash: 1 tablespoon horseradish plus ½ cup chopped fresh chives

Thai mash: Dissolve 1 tablespoon curry paste in a small amount of coconut milk; instead of mashing with rice or soy milk, use coconut milk (light is fine)

PIMPED MASHED POTATOES

Any fool can throw together mashed potatoes. But why settle for ho-hum when you can "pimp" your potatoes to Food Network standards with just a few easy additions? The possibilities are limitless. As I mentioned in my first cookbook, I religiously use a potato ricer to make mashed potatoes and other root veggies. It makes a creamier mash, plus it saves you the hassle of having to peel them, an especially important benefit during crazy-busy holidays like Thanksgiving.

1. If you plan on using a potato ricer, you can leave the potato skins on; otherwise peel the taters. Cut into quarters and boil for 10 to 15 minutes or until soft and mashable. (Alternatively, the potatoes can be microwaved until soft.)

2. Mash or rice the potatoes with Earth Balance and enough milk to reach the desired consistency. Sprinkle with salt and mix well.

3. Add your desired pimping ingredients. Adjust seasonings.

Yield: 4–6 servings, recipe is easily doubled

KWANZAA

The name Kwanzaa comes from a Swahili word which means "first fruits." It's an important holiday for African Americans and a reaffirmation of culture and identity. It takes place from December 26 to January 1. Like most holidays, Kwanzaa is focused on family, but it also brings into play community responsibility and self-improvement. It's an important time for reflection—and of course, for special foods.

MENU: FIRST FRUITS CELEBRATION

TANZANIAN CURRIED CHICKPEA-BANANA SOUP

$

This soup is traditionally made with chicken, but this kinder, gentler recipe features chickpeas. Seeing a banana in a savory dish is a fun surprise for us Westerners. I think the trend will catch on once you taste it.

1. Heat the oil over medium heat in a large stockpot. Add the onion and garlic and sauté until soft, about 5 minutes.
2. Stir in the curry, red pepper flakes, and black pepper and sauté for another minute or two.
3. Add everything else except the salt and the bananas. Bring to a boil and then reduce heat to low. Simmer partially covered for about 45 minutes.
4. Cut the bananas into chunks (about ½-inch dice) and add them to the pot. Simmer for 10 more minutes. Salt to taste.

Yield: 6 servings

2 tablespoons peanut oil

1 medium onion, chopped

4 cloves garlic, minced

2 tablespoons curry powder

2 teaspoons crushed red pepper flakes

1 teaspoon freshly ground black pepper

2 15-ounce cans chickpeas, rinsed and drained

6 cups vegetable stock

1 15-ounce can coconut milk (light is fine)

2 medium tomatoes, peeled and chopped

½ cup unsweetened grated coconut

About ¾ teaspoon salt, or to taste

2 ripe bananas

1 cup flour

1 cup cornmeal

3 tablespoons soy flour

5 tablespoons sugar

1 tablespoon nutritional yeast

½ teaspoon cinnamon

½ teaspoon salt

1 cup soy or rice milk

1 teaspoon apple cider vinegar

4 tablespoons (½ stick) Earth
  Balance, melted

1 cup corn, fresh or frozen

DOUBLE CORN BREAD

Traditionally the Kwanzaa table is decorated with, among other items, an ear of corn, which symbolizes children and the future. Moist, sweet bits of corn add a bit of dimension to this classic American quick bread. A hearty accompaniment to your Kwanzaa dinner, this corn bread is also wonderful for breakfast, warmed and slathered with Earth Balance and jam.

1. Preheat oven to 425°F. Grease a 9 x 9-inch pan.
2. Mix all dry ingredients in a large bowl.
3. Add wet ingredients and mix well. Stir in the corn.
4. Spoon batter into prepared pan. Bake for 20 to 25 minutes or until a cake tester comes out clean.
5. Cool on a rack and then cut into 9 squares or smaller squares.

Yield: 9 servings

SEITAN KEBABS WITH SMOKY YOGURT DIPPING SAUCE

These kebabs, with the accompanying dipping sauce, are a no-brainer for Kwanzaa. They're also awesome with the Cumin-Harissa Dipping Sauce (see page 166).

1. In a large bowl, mix together onion, lemon zest and juice, parsley, mint, salt, cumin, coriander, paprika, pepper, and olive oil. Add the seitan and toss to coat. Cover with plastic wrap and refrigerate for 2 to 4 hours, or overnight, stirring from time to time.
2. Preheat the grill or grill pan to high and lightly oil.
3. Skewer the seitan and place on the grill. Cook for about 10 to 20 minutes, turning evenly.
4. Remove seitan from skewers and serve with Smoky Yogurt Dipping Sauce.

Yield: 8 kebabs, or 4 servings

1 large red onion, finely chopped
1 tablespoon lemon zest
¼ cup fresh lemon juice
½ cup chopped fresh parsley
¼ cup chopped fresh mint
1 teaspoon salt
2 teaspoons cumin
1 teaspoon ground coriander
½ teaspoon sweet or smoked paprika
½ teaspoon freshly ground pepper
¼ cup olive oil
1 pound seitan, cut into 2-inch chunks
1 recipe Smoky Yogurt Dipping Sauce (see below)

SMOKY YOGURT DIPPING SAUCE

Cool with an earthy smokiness, this dipping sauce is the yin to the seitan kebab's yang. It also makes a tasty marinade for tofu or steamed tempeh.

Mix everything in a glass mason jar and shake well, or process in a blender or food processor.

Yield: 1 healthy cup

1 8-ounce container plain soy yogurt
1 garlic clove, crushed
1 teaspoon lemon zest
3 tablespoons tahini
½ teaspoon sesame oil
¼ teaspoon turmeric
1 teaspoon smoked Spanish paprika
1 tablespoon agave nectar
Pinch of cayenne pepper
Salt and pepper to taste

SWEET POTATO PIE WITH PECAN CRUST

Pie Filling

2 cups peeled and cubed sweet
  potatoes

1 cup sugar

1 teaspoon cinnamon

¼ teaspoon nutmeg

4 tablespoons (½ stick) Earth
  Balance, melted

¾ cup soy or rice milk

1 teaspoon vanilla

Pecan Crust

1 cup pecans

2 tablespoons Earth Balance,
  melted

2 tablespoons brown sugar

¼ cup whole pecan halves
  (optional)

This is an African-American and Southern classic. Comforting, sweet, and packing a powerful vitamin A punch, it's a wonderful way to end your Kwanzaa feast. If you're in an extra-decadent mood, top it with vanilla or dulce de leche soy ice cream. The pecan crust also works well with the 15-Minute Ice Cream Pie (see page 171).

1. Preheat oven to 375°F.
2. For the filling, boil sweet potatoes until soft, about 10 minutes, and drain well in a colander.
3. For the crust, pulse 1 cup pecans, Earth Balance, and brown sugar in a food processor until mixture sticks together just slightly in your hand.
4. Pour pecan mixture into a pie pan, and push down with your fingers to evenly cover the bottom and sides.
5. Using the food processor again, mix sweet potatoes, sugar, spices, and Earth Balance. Add milk and vanilla.
6. Pour filling into pie shell.
7. Decorate top with pecan halves, if desired.
8. Bake for 35 to 45 minutes or until a cake tester comes out fairly clean and the filling doesn't wobble.

Yield: 8 servings

FESTIVUS

If you're a Seinfeld fan—and who isn't?—you look forward to this episode more than Silk Soy Eggnog. Festivus started when Frank Costanza refused to conform to the status quo and decided to create a new holiday for those who were tired of the consumerism that goes hand-in-hand with the December holidays. And so "a Festivus for the rest of us" was born. It's the ultimate holiday for nonconformists. Instead of putting up a tree or lighting a menorah, the sole Festivus decoration is a simple aluminum pole. At the Festivus dinner, guests get a year's worth of anger off their chests during the "airing of grievances." The holiday is not officially over until the head of the family is wrestled and pinned in a ritual called the "feats of strength."

MENU: DINNER FOR THE REST OF US

CURRIED JERUSALEM ARTICHOKE VELOUTÉ

I won't lie to you, peeling all these little sunchokes is a feat of strength of its own. But once you taste this creamy, rich soup, you'll be glad you did.

1. In a large stockpot, melt Earth Balance over medium heat. Add onions and Jerusalem artichokes, and cook until onions are translucent, about 5 minutes.
2. Add potatoes, bouillon, half-and-half, wine, and curry powder. Heat until just about to boil.
3. Reduce heat to low, then cook uncovered for 20 to 25 minutes, or until potatoes and 'chokes are soft.
4. Carefully puree in a blender or with an immersion blender. Strain and serve warm.

Yield: 6 servings

2 tablespoons Earth Balance
1 onion, minced
2 pounds Jerusalem artichokes (also called sunchokes), peeled and cubed
2 medium potatoes, peeled and cubed
1 teaspoon Better Than Bouillon Vegetable, or equivalent of other vegetable bouillon
½ cup vegan half-and-half (or soy or rice milk, but half-and-half works best here)
⅓ cup dry white wine
1 teaspoon curry powder (Caribbean style, not Thai style)
Salt and pepper to taste

Salad

1 cup wild rice, cooked according to package directions*

⅔ cup dried cranberries

¾ cup very finely minced red onion

3 garlic cloves, crushed

1 cup cooked, shelled edamame

1 cup cooked corn (frozen is fine)

1 cup shredded carrot

1 cup chopped cilantro

Salt and pepper to taste

Dressing

2 tablespoons best-quality extra-virgin olive oil

2 tablespoons fresh-squeezed lemon juice

1 tablespoon maple syrup

2 teaspoons *ume* plum vinegar

1 teaspoon soy sauce

1 garlic clove, crushed

Pepper to taste

* Rice can be black, brown, or red rice from Camargue, or a combination for even more color. If you use a combination, cooking times can differ, so be sure to cook rice for the longest cooking time specified.

PRISMATIC WILD RICE SALAD

Yellow, green, magenta, black, yellow, orange, white. This colorful salad will make up for the starkness of the aluminum Festivus pole. This tastes best when left to marinate overnight. The cool thing? Besides being a feast for the eyes and super nutritious, this salad is also relatively low in fat.

1. In a large bowl, toss all of the salad ingredients.
2. In a medium bowl, whisk together all of the dressing ingredients.
3. Pour the dressing over the salad. Gently toss. Adjust seasonings. Refrigerate for at least 4 hours before serving, or preferably overnight.

Yield: 8 servings

Wine Pairing

Pour a soft, aromatic Verdejo from the Ruedo region of Spain.

Noochy Broccoli

Of course raw or lightly steamed vegetables are the most nutritious. This recipe, however, requires you to cook the heck out of the broccoli in order to achieve a pureed texture. So consider it a guilty veggie pleasure. Despite the mush factor, this cheesy broccoli mash is still a nutritional powerhouse (when compared, say, to the kinds of sad side dishes most people eat), and it will certainly fortify you for performing the feats of strength—or any time you need a little extra zing. This is also an excellent, simple-to-prepare topper for pasta and grains. Depending on how much olive oil you use (if any), this dish can range from no- or low-fat to mildly decadent.

Up to ½ cup vegetable broth
1 large bunch broccoli, cut into
    florets
5–6 cloves garlic, peeled
1 teaspoon soy sauce
Red pepper flakes (optional)
4–5 tablespoons nutritional yeast
Up to 1 tablespoon olive oil
    (optional)
Salt and pepper to taste

1. Bring about ¼ cup broth to a boil in a medium saucepan. Toss in broccoli, garlic, soy sauce, and red pepper, if using. Cover, lower heat to a simmer and steam-simmer for about 25 minutes or until completely mushy. (Check liquid level from time to time; you may need to add more broth.)
2. Pour the broccoli and its cooking liquid into a food processor. Sprinkle in nutritional yeast and begin processing. Depending on your preferences, add more broth and/or olive oil until this mash reaches your desired consistency. (For a thicker mash, pulse and don't add much liquid. For a saucier puree, process well and add enough liquid to make this puree smooth.)

Yield: 4 servings as a side

Variations

Substitute cauliflower, broccoli rabe, or Broccoflower for broccoli.

INTERNATIONAL CELEBRATIONS

To me, there is nothing more exciting than being in another country during a holiday, especially during a holiday unique to that land. Not only is it a privilege to witness, but it reveals more about the true nature of its citizens than you will ever uncover on an ordinary business day. Regardless of where you reside, we all share the very human desire to break bread with our family and friends on special days, whether they are religious, civic, or nationalistic. Try stepping outside your holiday comfort zone. Watch—and taste—how other people make a seemingly ordinary day extraordinary. It's cheaper than a plane ticket, and it's a wonderful journey.

Vesak

Vesak is the holiest Buddhist holiday celebrating the life, enlightenment, and death of the Buddha. It's a day of prayer and reflection. Temples are decorated with prayer flags and flowers, and birds and other caged animals are symbolically released in a gesture of generosity. On this day, devout Buddhists wear white, the color of respect, and also abstain from meat and share simple meals with those in need. Different countries have different names for this holiday. For example, in India, it's called Visakah Puja or Buddha Purnima; in Thailand it's called Visakha Bucha, and in Sri Lanka and Malaysia, it's known as Wesak. Vesak usually falls on the fourth full moon after the Lunar New Year, or the Sunday closest to that day.

MENU: BUDDHA'S DELIGHT

Naked Tofu

This is the quintessential Vesak recipe, so simple and innocent that I'm almost embarrassed to print it. "Naked tofu" is actually a misnomer, since the tofu does wear subtle "fig leaves" of flavor. I happen to love the taste of plain tofu, but eating this can be a Zen challenge to both omnivores and twenty-first-century herbivores who are used to the big, loud flavors of vegan convenience foods and vegan haute cuisine. The point is to remain in the present and experience the true essence of the tofu's texture and simplicity. Then maybe it will be easier to enjoy your own true essence.

Arrange the tofu in bowls. Sprinkle garlic and ginger over it, then drizzle with soy sauce to taste. Top with scallions and drizzle with sesame oil.

Yield: 4 servings

1 16-ounce block extra-firm tofu, uncooked, cut into bite-sized cubes or triangles
2 garlic cloves, crushed
1-inch piece ginger, peeled and grated
2–4 tablespoons best-quality soy sauce (I recommend Nama Shoyu)
½ cup sliced scallions
Sesame oil for drizzling

RAMEN NOODLE BOWL

6 cups vegetable stock

1 large onion, sliced

3 cups sliced green cabbage

2 garlic cloves, sliced

1-inch piece ginger, peeled and grated

1 carrot, very thinly sliced

½ cup chopped button, shiitake, and/or maitake mushrooms

1 cup broccoli florets

½ cup shelled edamame

2–4 tablespoons soy sauce (depending on your taste and the sodium content of the broth)

1 pound ramen noodles or vermicelli

½–1 teaspoon salt

2 teaspoons sesame oil

½ cup sliced scallions

Remember those four-for-a-dollar ramen noodle soup packs? I—shudder! —lived on them in my early twenties. Yes, they're cheap and simple, but most are also loaded with sodium, hydrogenated oils, and unpronounceable preservatives. Ramen noodles are a snap to prepare at home. Fast, frugal, and perfect for sharing.

1. In a large stockpot, bring broth to a boil. Add ginger and vegetables, reduce heat, cover, and simmer until vegetables are tender, about 15 minutes.
2. Add noodles and cook according to the package directions until done but still firm. Season with salt to taste.
3. Arrange in bowls. Drizzle with sesame oil and soy sauce to taste and garnish with scallions.

Yield: 4–6 servings

Variations

Add ½ cup of any of the following: Dry-Fried Tofu (see page 82), seitan chunks, bean sprouts, spring peas, or corn kernels.

STICKY RICE WITH MANGO

This is one of my all-time favorite desserts, and I indulge just about every time I visit a Thai restaurant. Besides tasting fabulous, this sweet ending relies on very basic ingredients and is a snap to put together. It also presents beautifully, especially if you mold the rice in a ramekin or other shaped mold before plating it. My friendly neighborhood Thai restaurant uses a heart-shaped mold, which also makes this a perfect Valentine's Day or anniversary dessert.

1½ cups dry white rice
2½ cups water
1 14- to 15-ounce can coconut milk (full fat tastes best, but low fat also works)
1 cup sugar
1 teaspoon vanilla
¼ teaspoon salt
3 mangos, peeled and sliced
1 tablespoon toasted sesame seeds (black, white, or a combination)

1. Cook rice in water according to package directions. Fluff with a fork.
2. In a large saucepan, heat coconut milk, sugar, vanilla, and salt over medium heat, stirring well until sugar is dissolved.
3. Pour half of the coconut milk mixture over the rice and mix until just coated.
4. If molding, divide mixture among ramekins or molds lightly sprayed with cooking spray and press rice in firmly. Refrigerate for at least an hour. Turn out onto a plate and proceed to step 6.
5. If not molding, arrange ⅙ of rice on each plate.
6. Arrange sliced mango around the rice, sprinkle with sesame seeds, then drizzle with some of the remaining sauce.

Yield: 6 servings

Wine Pairing

Moscato d'Asti, a tropical fruit-scented frizzante wine from Italy's Piedmont region, is slightly sparkling, lightly sweet, and low in alcohol.

TIMKAT

Timkat, or Ethiopian Epiphany, falls on January 19 (or January 20 in a leap year) and is the most lavish holiday in Ethiopia. During this three-day festival, which celebrates the gifts of the three kings, Ethiopians dress in white and parade a replica of the Ark of the Covenant while accompanied by the sound of beating drums. In the wee hours of the morning, celebrants attend mass and a group baptism.

MENU: ETHIOPIAN EPIPHANY FEAST

ETHIOPIAN COLLARDS

1 pound collards, thick center stalks removed

2 tablespoons peanut or canola oil

1 medium red onion, chopped very finely

½ teaspoon salt or less to taste (you may not need any if you are using a salted broth)

3 garlic cloves, crushed

1½-inch piece ginger, peeled and grated

1 long hot green pepper, seeded and chopped very finely

1 cup reserved collard-boiling water or vegetable stock

Freshly ground pepper to taste

Lemon wedges (optional)

Collards are so healthy and filling, and they stand up nicely to the assertive heat of the ginger and hot pepper. Finish them off with a squeeze of fresh lemon juice.

1. Chop collards as finely as possible. A mezzaluna is the perfect tool for this.
2. Boil collards for about 10 to 15 minutes. Drain and press out as much excess water as possible, reserving water (if you can remember).
3. Heat oil in large sauté pan over medium heat. Sauté onions until they just start to brown. Sprinkle with salt, then add garlic, ginger, and pepper. Cook for another 3 or 4 minutes.
4. Add water/stock and collards to the pan. Cover and cook for about 20 minutes, or until everything is soft. (Check at about 10 minutes and add more water/stock, if needed.)
5. Adjust seasonings. Squeeze lemons over collards, if using, and serve over rice or mini *injeras* (page 63).

Yield: 4 servings

MINI INJERAS

Smart Cars. Miniskirts. Haiku. Good things come in small packages. Since space is limited in my petite urban kitchen, I decided to downsize traditional LP-sized *injera* bread to a more manageable pancake round. Topped with spicy, ginger-infused collards, this dish also makes an elegant appetizer or light summer meal. I recommend using a nonstick skillet for these.

1½–2 cups water
2 cups teff flour
1 tablespoon vinegar
½ teaspoon salt, or more to taste
Canola or peanut oil for frying
(if you're not using a nonstick skillet)

1. In a large bowl, starting with 1½ cups water, whisk together all ingredients except oil until smooth. Depending on humidity, you may need to add more water. Batter should be a tad thicker than pancake batter. Set aside for at least 15 minutes.
2. Heat about 1 tablespoon oil in a cast-iron skillet over medium. Spread ¼ of the batter with a spoon and shape into a round.
3. Cook until bubbles start to form. Flip and cook on the other side until firm.
4. Remove pancake, then repeat with the remaining batter.

Yield: 4 mini flatbreads

SPICED LENTILS

4 tablespoons canola oil

Spice Mixture

⅛ teaspoon cardamom seeds
¼ teaspoon red pepper flakes
Pinch ground nutmeg
3 black peppercorns
I whole clove
Pinch of turmeric
¼ teaspoon cumin seeds

2 cups seeded and chopped
   Anaheim, cubanelle, or
   Hungarian peppers
4 cloves garlic, minced
2 large onions, chopped
I½-inch piece ginger, peeled and
   minced
½ teaspoon salt, or to taste
I pound (2 cups) brown lentils,
   rinsed and picked over
4 cups vegetable broth

Since they are inherently warming and filling, lentils are a no-brainer winter dish. The heat of the ginger and warming spices bump up the comfort factor even more. Don't be intimidated by the long list of ingredients for the spice mixture. This recipe is easier than it looks.

1. In a large, high-sided frying pan or Dutch oven, heat oil over medium heat. Toss in spice mixture and let heat for a minute or two.
2. Add peppers, garlic, onion, and ginger, and sauté for about 10 to 15 minutes, or until soft. Sprinkle with salt.
3. Add lentils and cook for about I minute.
4. Add broth and bring to a boil.
5. Cover and reduce heat to low. Cook, covered, for about 45 minutes to I hour, or until lentils are soft. Stir occasionally, and add more water or broth as needed.

Yield: 4–6 servings

Cinco de Mayo

For many people of a certain age, this holiday exists for the sole purpose of consuming mass quantities of tequila. But for the rest of us, it's an excuse to pull out our Lila Downs CDs and dive into mass quantities of Mexican food. (Okay. With at least a little splash of tequila.)

MENU: FIESTA MEXICANA

Easy Watermelon Daiquiri

Serve this gorgeous libation in a sugar-rimmed margarita glass, garnished with a few berries. Careful: It's addictive.

Process all ingredients in a blender. That's it.

Yield: 4 servings

2 cups seeded watermelon
    chunks
Juice of ½ lime
6 ounces tequila
3 ounces Cointreau
1–2 tablespoons agave nectar
    (depending on how sweet the
    watermelon is)

Enlightened Guacamole

I love guacamole, but it can be too rich and can scare away your fat-phobic friends. Since peas are fairly bland, adding them is a good way to "thin out" the guacamole, plus they color coordinate nicely with the avocados.

    Now everyone likes their guac how they like it. That said, think of this recipe merely as a starting point. Play with the proportions of spice, lime juice, and garlic until you're happy.

Gently pulse everything together in the food processor. Be careful not to overprocess (unless, of course, you are militant about disguising the peas). Serve as a condiment or with crudités or corn chips.

Yield: About 2 cups

1 medium plum tomato, seeded
    and chopped fine
1 cup frozen peas, thawed (I know
    this sounds like an oxymoron!)
1 avocado, pitted, flesh scooped out
3 tablespoons lime juice
¼ cup minced fresh cilantro
1 small jalapeño, stemmed, seeded,
    and finely minced
1 tablespoon finely minced onion
2 garlic cloves, crushed
¼–½ teaspoon chipotle pepper
    powder
¼ teaspoon cumin
Salt and pepper to taste

1 tablespoon olive oil

1 onion, chopped

3 garlic cloves, crushed

2 15-ounce cans chickpeas, rinsed
and drained (about 4 cups)

1 16-ounce jar salsa verde or
tomatillo salsa

½–1 teaspoon chili powder (I like
ancho or chipotle)

¼ teaspoon cayenne pepper

Salt and pepper to taste

¼ cup chopped fresh cilantro

About ½ cup vegan sour cream
for garnish

Avocado slices for garnish

SHAMEFULLY SIMPLE
CHICKPEA CHILI

At the risk of stepping on Sandra Lee's (of TV's *Semi-Homemade* fame) turf, this dish is bona fide semi-homemade. But it's also yummy and perfect for Cinco de Mayo parties. Plus, it's a no-brainer when you're craving some protein but don't feel like digging out your favorite all-out chili recipe. I love the color contrast between the blond chickpeas and the verdant salsa verde. Serve this with warmed corn chips or corn tortillas or over a bed of Spanish rice.

1.   Heat oil in a medium casserole pan over medium heat. Add onions and garlic and sauté until translucent, about 5 minutes.
2.   Mix chickpeas, salsa, and spices in a large saucepan. Bring to a boil, then lower to a simmer and heat for about 20 to 25 minutes, or until warmed through. (Add a bit of broth halfway through if mixture seems too thick for your taste.)
3.   Adjust seasonings. Top with cilantro and sour cream and/or avocado slices, if desired.

Yield: 6 servings

Variation

Replace chickpeas with any bean: pintos, black beans, kidney beans.

FAJITAS

Fajitas are fun to make and eat. If you're having a party, you can set up a topping bar, and guests can assemble their own fajitas, freeing up your time to pour yourself more tequila!

1. Heat oil in a large sauté pan over medium heat. Sauté the onion until translucent, then add the seitan, pepper strips, and mushrooms. Cover and sauté until soft, stirring occasionally, about 10 more minutes.
2. Stir in spices and broth. Bring to a boil.
3. Reduce heat to low. Cook for about 5 minutes or until broth cooks down a bit and mixture thickens.
4. Stir in cilantro. Divide among tortillas and serve. Let guests add toppings as desired.

Yield: 4 fajitas; recipe is easily doubled or tripled

Variations

You can simply skip the seitan and add more mushrooms. You can also substitute ¾ cup pressed, extra-firm tofu for the seitan.

1 tablespoon olive oil

1 medium onion, sliced

¾ cup seitan strips

1 red pepper, seeded and cut into strips

1 cup sliced mushrooms

½ teaspoon chili powder, or to taste

1 teaspoon cumin

⅓ cup vegetable broth

¼ cup chopped fresh cilantro

Salt and pepper to taste

6 flour tortillas, warmed (experiment with different varieties: red chili. spinach, whole grain)

Optional toppings: guacamole (see page 65); vegan sour cream; salsa; Daiya cheddar cheese; nutritional yeast; cooked corn; cooked, shelled edamame; sliced scallions

5 medium tomatoes, seeded and
diced

1 jalapeño pepper, seeded and
very finely minced

1 mango, peeled, seeded, and
diced

1 peach, peeled and diced

1 avocado, peeled, pitted, and
diced

⅓ cup pineapple, diced

½ cup corn (frozen is fine)

15 green grapes, quartered

½ cup chopped fresh cilantro

3 cloves garlic, minced

½ teaspoon salt, or to taste

3 tablespoons fresh lime juice

⅓ cup chopped red onion

3 tablespoons olive oil

FRUITY SALSA

The abundance of fruit in this festive salsa (and yes, tomatoes are technically fruits, not vegetables) tempers the heat of the chili, onions, and garlic. It's a great topper for the Fajitas (see page 67) or burritos. But I love it best dumped atop extra-large yellow corn chips.

Mix everything in a large glass bowl. Allow to sit for several hours before serving, or preferably overnight.

Yield: 6 servings

BASTILLE DAY

You don't have to be French to storm the proverbial meat-centric Bastille and celebrate the power of kindness. These French recipes are quite democratic and will please *citoyens* of both human and animal persuasions.

MENU: REVOLUTIONARY FEAST

PÂTÉ AUX CHAMPIGNONS ÉXOTIQUES (EXOTIC MUSHROOM PÂTÉ)

When I was recently in Paris to give a cooking demonstration at Paris Vegan Day, I fell in love with the numerous vegan pâtés for sale in health food stores and supermarkets across the city. Serve this spread on a freshly baked, whole grain baguette.

1. In a medium sauté pan, heat 1 tablespoon oil over medium heat. Add onion and sauté until soft, about 5 minutes. Add mushrooms and cook until soft, about 10 to 15 minutes.
2. Place the onion-mushroom mixture in a food processor and process with the yeast, potato flour, and salt and pepper until very smooth. Add more olive oil in ½-tablespoon increments if mixture seems too thick. (If you are want to cut down on fat, add vegetable broth instead. Just be sure to reduce the amount of salt or omit it altogether if the broth has added salt.)

Yield: About ½ cup

2–3 tablespoons olive oil
½ small onion, chopped
½ cup flavorful mushrooms (shiitake, chanterelles, oyster, or a combination; whole, sliced, or coarsely chopped)
3 tablespoons nutritional yeast
1 tablespoon potato flour (substitute cornstarch if you cannot find it)
¼ teaspoon sea salt, or to taste
Freshly ground pepper
Vegetable broth for thinning (optional)

ONIONS MONEGASQUE

½ pound small white onions, peeled

3 tablespoons olive oil

1 tomato, peeled, seeded, and chopped fine

½ cup white vinegar

⅓ cup raisins

½ teaspoon dried thyme

1 tablespoon chopped fresh parsley

1 garlic clove, minced

1 tablespoon sugar

Pinch of nutmeg

Up to 2 cups broth

Slow, methodical cooking helps transform this set of humble ingredients into a super-elegant recipe. Serve with bread, toast, or crackers.

This recipe actually hails from Monaco, and not from France, per se, but since (warning: historical aside) the French Revolutionary forces took control of Monaco in 1793, and since it stayed under French control until the early 1800s, I think it's close enough.

1. Bring a pot of water to a boil. Blanch the onions and then immediately drain them and rinse them with cold water to stop the cooking. Set aside.
2. Heat the oil in a large sauté pan over medium-high heat. Sauté the onions until browned and soft, stirring constantly, about 8 minutes.
3. Add tomato, vinegar, raisins, herbs, garlic, sugar, nutmeg, and 1 cup of broth. Bring to a boil. Reduce heat to a simmer and cook for about 1 hour, adding more broth from time to time as the liquid cooks off.
4. Raise heat to high and deglaze the pan, removing as much liquid as possible without burning the ingredients. Remove from heat, place in a dish, and serve.

Yield: 4–6 servings

TOFU DIJON

Just as it's a myth that you can't bake without eggs, it's also a myth that all French food is complicated. This dish, for one, is super simple. It exudes a certain elegance that only best-quality Dijon mustard can impart. This is especially nice accompanied with a dab of Easy Aioli (see page 127). Serve it with sweet green beans or a frisée or mesclun salad.

1. Preheat oven to 350°F.
2. Sprinkle tofu with salt.
3. Heat oil over medium heat in a large sauté pan. Add garlic, mustard, and wine, and cook gently until garlic is soft, taking care not to burn it, about 3 to 4 minutes. The point here is to infuse the oil with mustard and garlic flavors. Add the pressed tofu to the pan, and stir, being sure to coat all sides.
4. Mix bread crumbs, herbes de Provence, paprika, and pepper in a shallow bowl. Dredge each piece of tofu in the bread crumb mixture.
5. Place tofu on a greased or greased and foil-lined baking sheet. Bake for 15 minutes on each side, or until browned.

Yield: 4 servings

1 pound extra-firm tofu, pressed and cut into 4 steaks (see pressing directions, page xi)
1 teaspoon salt
2 tablespoons olive oil
4 garlic cloves, minced
3 tablespoons Dijon mustard (please use the real deal; it will make a difference)
3 tablespoons dry white wine
1½ cups bread crumbs
1 tablespoon herbes de Provence
¼ teaspoon paprika
Freshly ground pepper to taste

TARTELETTES AU CITRON (LITTLE LEMON TARTS)

Lemon Filling

1 12.3-ounce aseptic box extra-firm silken tofu (do not use refrigerated tofu; it will be too grainy and will not taste right)

2⅔ cups confectioners' sugar, plus more for dusting

½ cup fresh-squeezed lemon juice

2 tablespoons very finely grated lemon zest

2 tablespoons cornstarch

½ teaspoon salt

Pâte Sucrée

1¼ cups flour

¼ cup sugar

½ cup (1 stick) nonhydrogenated vegan shortening

1 teaspoon vanilla or lemon extract

1 tablespoon very finely grated lemon zest

¼ teaspoon salt

1–2 tablespoons water

Fresh raspberries or strawberries for garnish (optional)

Ooh là là! What would a Bastille Day celebration be without a puckery lemon tart to finish off your meal? There's something elegant about the subtle sweet and sour combination that pairs very nicely with a cup of tea. Aside from rolling out the dough, this is a very easy recipe to prepare. You can make these as individual tarts, which I think present much nicer. Or make one large tart and add about 15 minutes or so to the baking time.

1. For the filling, whiz everything together in a food processor until absolutely smooth; better to overprocess than to underwhiz. Pour into a dish and refrigerate until you're going to use. (You can make this up to one day ahead of time.) Clean out the food processor, because you'll need it to make the crust.

2. For the pâte sucrée, pulse everything together except the water in the food processor. Stir in the water, ½ tablespoon at a time, until the dough just sticks together. If it seems a little sticky, don't stress. As long as it holds together between your fingers, it's fine.

3. Refrigerate dough for at least 2 hours.

4. Preheat the oven to 350°F.

5. On a lightly floured surface, roll out the dough to your desired size. Place the dough into the individual tartlet pans or in one larger tart pan.

6. Fill the pastry-lined pans with the lemon mixture, leaving at least ¼ inch of headspace, since the filling will rise a bit in the oven.

7. Bake tartlets for 25 to 30 minutes, or until they are no longer watery and wobbly. If making the larger tart, bake it about 40 to 45 minutes or until no longer watery and wobbly.

8. Cool on a rack for 5 minutes. Chill completely before serving. Dust with confectioners' sugar just before serving. Garnish with a raspberry or sliced strawberry, if desired.

Yield: 12 tartlets or 1 large tart

EARTH DAY

This holiday is like Mother's Day for Mama Earth. Celebrating the planet with a fancy vegan feast is the surest way to show the earth—and your family—how much you care. The first Earth Day was held in the United States on April 22, 1970, and now it's celebrated in more than 175 countries. It's held on April 22, the equinox, marking the first day of spring in the Northern Hemisphere, and the first day of fall in the Southern Hemisphere. My feast includes seasonal foods from both halves of the globe.

MENU: EARTH DAY FEAST

CHILLED PEA SOUP WITH MINT AND GARLIC SCAPES

In the Northern Hemisphere, garlic scapes are one of the first signs of spring. This celadon soup is a refreshing juxtaposition of flavors: sweet peas, perky mint, and a hint of mild heat from the garlic scapes. Best of all, it's super simple to make. Prepare it in the morning before you leave for work, so it can chill all day in the refrigerator, then puree it just before serving.

6 cups vegetable stock
1 16-ounce bag frozen petite peas
1 bunch garlic scapes (about 5 or 6 stalks), cut into 1-inch pieces
1 cup mint leaves, plus extra for garnish
1 6-ounce container plain soy yogurt
½ cup plain soy milk
Salt and pepper to taste
Extra-virgin olive oil or walnut oil (optional)

1. In a large pot, bring stock to a boil. Add peas, garlic scapes, and mint. Boil gently for about 10 to 15 minutes. Whisk in yogurt and soy milk.
2. Chill in refrigerator for at least 4 hours or overnight. Puree just before serving and garnish with a few fresh mint leaves. Drizzle with a bit of extra-virgin olive oil or walnut oil, if desired.

Yield: 8 servings

FARFALLE WITH SHALLOTS AND CHARD

3–4 tablespoons extra-virgin olive oil

¼ teaspoon hot pepper flakes

5–6 shallots, peeled and sliced into rings (enough to equal approximately 1 medium onion)

1 teaspoon salt

1 large bunch chard, tough stems removed, leaves very finely chopped

1 pound farfalle (good substitutes include orecchiette and gemelli)

About 1 tablespoon fresh lemon juice

Nutritional yeast for sprinkling

In my opinion, shallots are one of the most neglected veggies in America. Often overshadowed by their bolder cousins, onion and garlic, the classy shallot has a gentler, sweeter taste. In some ways, though, its subtlety is more powerful and enduring. Think of Audrey Hepburn in a bulb. In this easy dish, I've paired shallots with another spring classic, chard, with a bit of lemon juice for freshness.

1. Bring a large pot of salted water to a boil.
2. Heat oil over medium heat in a large high-sided pan. Add hot pepper flakes, let cook for a few seconds to infuse the oil, then add the shallots. Sprinkle with salt, and sauté until the shallots are soft and translucent, about 5 to 10 minutes. Take care not to brown them.
3. Meanwhile, blanch the chard in the boiling water just until it wilts. The idea is simply to precook the greens; be careful not to overcook them or you will have mush (and fewer vitamins). Depending on the variety of chard you use, it will color your water from beet red to dark green. This is normal and will add even more flavor to your pasta as it cooks.
4. Remove chard with a slotted spoon and drain it in a colander. (Keep the water at a boil.) When it's cool enough to handle, squeeze out any excess water.
5. Add pasta to your colored water. Cook according to package directions.
6. Turn up the heat under the shallots-pepper-oil mixture and add a ladle of pasta water, then stir in the chard and lemon juice. Add more water if it seems dry (or more oil, if you are prone to decadence).
7. When chard is cooked through (taste first!), toss with drained farfalle, top with nutritional yeast and more salt, if desired, and enjoy.

Yield: 4–6 servings

EARTHY EGGPLANT

This versatile recipe borrows from North African, European, and Mediterranean culinary traditions. It's perfect for using up the fruits of your summer co-op harvest and works well as a dip, side dish, or as a main, served over any whole grain or pasta. Try it over the Golden Millet Pilaf (see page 125).

1. Preheat oven to 400°F. Cover a cookie sheet with a lightly oiled piece of foil.
2. Prick the eggplants all over with a fork. Place the eggplants on the cookie sheet. Roast until completely pooped, about 1 hour. (Time will depend on the size of your eggplants.) Remove from oven and cool completely before handling.
3. Meanwhile, heat the oil in a large saucepan over medium heat. Add the raisins, mushrooms, onion, and garlic and sauté until soft and most of the cooking liquid is absorbed, about 10 to 15 minutes.
4. When the eggplants are cool enough to handle, cut them in half and scoop out the insides. Mix this with the sautéed veggies and remaining ingredients either in a large bowl by hand if you prefer a chunkier texture, or in a food processor or blender of you prefer a smoother texture. If mixture seems dry, add more olive oil. Adjust seasonings.
5. However you decide to eat it, top it with toasted pine nuts and drizzle with extra-virgin olive oil.

Yield: About 4 cups

2 medium eggplants
1 tablespoon olive oil
⅓ cup raisins or sultanas (golden raisins)
½ cup sliced mushrooms (your choice)
1 medium onion, diced
4–5 garlic cloves, sliced
⅓ cup fresh lemon juice
2 teaspoons ground cumin
½ teaspoon paprika
3 tablespoons nutritional yeast
½–1 teaspoon salt
¼ cup fresh chopped parsley
2–3 tablespoons chopped fresh mint
Freshly ground pepper to taste
½ cup toasted pine nuts
Extra-virgin olive oil for drizzling

Variations

For a creamier dip, add about 2 tablespoons or so) of plain soy yogurt.
Optional additions (add in step 3): ½ cup chopped sun-dried tomatoes,
½ cup chopped black or green olives. Drizzle with pomegranate molasses.

Wine Pairing

Rosé from either the French or Italian side of the Mediterranean
will easily handle the sweet-salty-spicy of this dish.

World Vegetarian Day

On October 1, World Vegetarian Day kicks off a month-long celebration of vegetarian food and its resulting win-win benefits for animals, the planet, and our health. This celebratory vegan feast centers on healthy, colorful foods created from the abundant late-summer and early-autumn harvest.

MENU: VEGGIE FEAST

1 cup squash or pumpkin seeds
1 tablespoon Earth Balance
½ cup sugar, brown or white
1½ teaspoons dried rosemary
½ teaspoon ground cumin
½ teaspoon dried oregano
¼ teaspoon salt

Candied Squash Seeds

Save those seeds. Besides being tasty, toasted squash and pumpkin seeds are also high in protein, minerals, and fiber. Plus, I just love the idea of using a vegetable so thoroughly. It makes me feel like a pioneer woman.

If you're pressed for time, you can simply toast the seeds in the oven and sprinkle them with sea salt. But adding this simple, sweet-hot coating—with its earthy cumin undertone—elevates this humble staple into bona fide party fare.

1. After scooping out squash or pumpkin seeds, remove by hand as much of the fibrous pulp as you can. Then soak the seeds in a bowl of water and give them a few whirls. The seeds will float, and most of the pulp will sink. Drain and dry off seeds as best you can, without getting too obsessive. Spread them out on a cookie sheet sprayed with cookie spray and let them dry out for about an hour, or longer, if you have time.
2. Preheat oven to 350°F.
3. Place seeds in the oven and toast until golden, about 8 to 10 minutes.
4. Melt the Earth Balance in a small saucepan, preferably cast iron, over low heat. Turn heat up to medium high and stir in the remaining ingredients until well blended. The mixture will be very clumpy; this is normal.
5. Add the seeds. Crank up the heat slightly and stir continually. After about 5 to 7 minutes, the sugar will caramelize and begin clinging to the seeds. Keep stirring and be careful not to burn. Once they have a candy coating that seems to harden, remove the pan from heat and transfer back to the cookie sheet to prevent further browning. Spread out the seeds and let them harden at room temperature.

Yield: About 1 cup; recipe is easily doubled

Pop!
When you're toasting squash seeds, you might hear a little party in your oven.
Don't be alarmed: Squash seeds pop when exposed to high heat.

CECINA (CHICKPEA FLATBREADS)

These little chickpea flatbreads seem so exotic, yet they are a snap to make. Plus, they're much healthier and lower in fat than store-bought chips. Serve these soft wedges with Smoky Zucchini Bean Dip (see page 79), Lazy Bean Dip (see page 35), Enlightened Guacamole (see page 65), hummus, or anything else savory and scoopable.

2–3 teaspoons olive oil

I cup chickpea (gram) flour, plus extra if necessary

I cup vegetable broth

I tablespoon dried basil

Dash of salt

Dash of freshly ground black pepper

1. Preheat oven to 400°F. Brush a large, deep cookie sheet with the olive oil.
2. In a large bowl, mix remaining ingredients with a wire whisk until no lumps remain. Batter should be fairly thick. If it seems too thin, add more flour, I tablespoon at a time
3. Pour batter onto pan and flatten the top gently with a spatula sprayed with cooking spray. Bake for 6 to 10 minutes, or until golden.
4. Remove from oven and let cool for a few minutes. Break into pieces and serve.

Yield: 6 servings

MILLET-STUFFED MUSHROOMS WITH AIOLI

4 large portobello caps
4 teaspoons olive oil
Salt and pepper to taste
½ recipe Golden Millet Pilaf (see page 125)
1 recipe Easy Aioli (see page 127)

I love the earthy-woody flavor of portobello mushrooms. Stuff them with sweet-salty millet and top with a healthy dollop of creamy aioli, and the juxtaposition of all those flavors is heaven to the palate.

This elegant dish presents beautifully, even if you're not a certified food stylist. It's a true celebration of vegan haute cuisine.

1. Preheat the oven to 475°F. Clean the mushrooms by gently removing the gills and the stem. (Save them for the next time you're making broth from scratch.) Rub the insides and the edges of each cap with 1 teaspoon oil. Season with salt and pepper.
2. Place the mushroom caps on a lightly oiled cookie tray and bake for 15 to 20 minutes, or until caps are soft.
3. Stuff each cap with a mound of pilaf (about ½ cup or so, depending on the size of the mushroom). Top with a generous dollop of aioli and serve.

Yield: 4 servings

Wine Pairing

"Meaty" mushrooms like portobellos can handle a little tannin, so try a medium-bodied Piemontese Dolcetto from either Alba or Dogliani.

SMOKY ZUCCHINI BEAN DIP

Since it happily absorbs flavors much like tofu does, zucchini makes a great flavor and fiber base. This easy, speckled dip marries smokiness from the hummus and smoked Spanish paprika, and bright citrus notes from the lemon juice and sumac (an herb that you can find in most Middle Eastern groceries). Serve it with pita bread, crostini, or crudités. It also makes a fantastic sandwich spread. Try it on panini with tomatoes and olives.

Combine everything in the food processor and process until the dip reaches your desired consistency. If the dip is too thick, add water or broth in 1 tablespoon increments.

Yield: 2 healthy cups

1 medium zucchini, sliced into 2-inch rounds

1 15- to 16-ounce can pinto beans, rinsed and drained

1–2 garlic cloves, sliced

5 tablespoons tahini

Juice of ½ lemon

½ teaspoon smoked Spanish paprika

2 teaspoons sumac

½ teaspoon salt

Freshly ground pepper to taste

SAVORY HARVEST CRUMBLE WITH FIGS, SQUASH, AND CELERIAC

1 medium winter squash (e.g., kabocha, butternut, acorn—don't worry too much about amount)

1 tablespoon olive oil

Dash of salt plus ½ teaspoon

2 medium celeriacs (also called celery root)

½ teaspoon lemon juice

1 tablespoon maple syrup

1 medium red onion, diced

1 cup de-stemmed and chopped dried Calimyrna figs

Crumble Topping

¾ cup rolled oats

⅓ cup chopped walnuts

¼ cup (½ stick) Earth Balance

½ teaspoon cinnamon

Normally, we associate crumbles with fruits, but the ideas of a moist compote covered by a crumbly topping translates beautifully to the cornucopia of autumn vegetables available in early fall. This dish is a bit time consuming, so I suggest cooking the squash and making the topping ahead of time if you can.

1. Preheat oven to 400°F. Line a cookie sheet with foil.
2. Cut squash in half and deseed it. (Save seeds for Candied Squash Seeds, see page 76.) Rub the insides with olive oil and sprinkle with salt. Bake for about 30 to 45 minutes or until soft (cooking time will vary, depending on the squash you use). Remove from the oven and let cool. Once cool, scoop out the soft interior.
3. Meanwhile, peel celeriacs and cut into ½-inch dice. Place in a small saucepan filled with water. Add lemon juice. Bring to a boil and boil for about 10 minutes, or until soft. Remove from heat and set aside. Do not drain yet.
4. In a large bowl, mix together the squash, maple syrup, onion, figs, and ½ teaspoon salt. Drain celeriac and add to the mixture.
5. To make the crumble topping, mix the ingredients together in a small bowl, using your fingers to crumble everything together thoroughly.
6. Spread the squash mixture into a greased 9 x 9-inch pan.
7. Randomly sprinkle the crumble mixture over the squash filling.
8. Bake for 40 to 50 minutes or until topping is golden.

Yield: 6 servings as a side

DIWALI

This major Hindu holiday celebrates Rama and Sita's return to their home after fourteen years of exile and is a testament to good prevailing over evil. This festival is celebrated for five days. People clean and decorate their homes and share gifts and sweets with loved ones and friends. People dress up in their newest, fanciest clothes and purchase new utensils. Both the young—and the young at heart—enjoy the spectacular firework displays that mark this feast.

MENU: INDIAN SWEETS FOR RAMA AND SITA

SAG PANEER

You need to line your stomach with something nutritious before indulging in all those fabulous Diwali sweets. Your kitchen will smell so fragrant when you're making this easy *sag paneer*. This recipe uses pantry staples, and the paneer is made from pressed, dry-fried tofu. Feel free to play around with the spice proportions to adjust to your personal preferences. (I, for example, would toss in at least ¾ teaspoon red pepper flakes! But I have a real "heat tooth.") Serve over brown basmati rice or, for a change, cooked millet or barley.

1. Process onion, garlic, and ginger in a food processor until they almost reach a paste consistency.
2. Heat oil in medium saucepan over medium heat. Sauté the onion mixture until soft and heated through, about 5 minutes. Add spices to the pan. Stir everything to coat and cook another 5 minutes. Mixture will be very thick and will stick together.
3. Add spinach. Stir to coat with the spice/onion mixture. Stir in half-and-half and add tofu "paneer."
4. Cover and cook over medium-low heat for about 30 minutes, stirring occasionally. Mixture should be at a tiny, gentle boil.
5. Add salt to taste. Remove from heat and let cool for about 5 minutes before serving.

Yield: 4 servings

1 pound extra-firm tofu, cut into small cubes and dry-fried (see directions for Dry-Fried Tofu, page 82)
1 red onion, roughly chopped
6 garlic cloves, halved
1 1-inch piece ginger, peeled and lightly chopped
1 pound frozen, chopped organic spinach, thawed
1 tablespoon olive oil
2 teaspoons garam masala
1½ teaspoons ground cumin
½ teaspoon ground coriander
¼ teaspoon red pepper flakes
¼ teaspoon turmeric
1 cinnamon stick
½ cup vegan half-and-half if you are using frozen spinach, ¾ cup if you are using fresh
Up to ½ teaspoon salt, or to taste

Variation

Sag Chana Paneer: Add a 15-ounce can of rinsed and drained chickpeas along with the spinach and tofu in step 3.

DRY-FRIED TOFU

1 pound extra-firm tofu

This pressed, dry-fried protein has the chewy texture of fried tofu, but with no added fat. It's extremely versatile, and when properly dressed up, it can turn avid tofu haters into tofu lovers. Dry-Fried Tofu has a featured role in Sag Paneer (see page 81), but its possibilities are limitless. Add dry-fried cubes to your favorite curry coconut sauce along with cooked veggies. Coat them with your favorite barbecue, teriyaki, or satay sauce, and bake and serve over brown rice. Toss into salads. Cut cubes larger, skewer, and grill, served with Yogurt-Tahini Sauce (see page 137). Or just eat them plain, with a minimal squirt of soy sauce and scallions, as I've been known to do when I get the munchies.

1. First, press the tofu. Leave it whole and wrap tofu in tea towels or paper towels. Place it between two large plates and weight down with two very large books. After 1 hour, replace towels with dry ones and flip. Press for 1 more hour. Cut into desired shapes, such as large or small cubes or triangles.

2. To dry-fry the tofu, heat a frying pan to medium-high heat. Do not add any oil. Place the pressed tofu on the pan. Do not crowd the pan. Cook for a minute or so on each side, or until just golden brown. Flip and repeat until all sides are cooked and golden brown. Set aside and repeat with remaining tofu.

Yield: 4 servings

CLEMENTINE–SWEET POTATO HALWAH

Everyone loves a more traditional, carrot-based *halwah*. But then again, everyone also loves a little innovation. This *halwah* is something of an Indian-American fusion recipe, using starchy sweet potatoes instead of carrots, and clementines for an unexpected, gentle citrus bite. But it still contains the nuts, dried fruit, and warming spices used in a more traditional *halwah*.

1. Preheat oven to 400°F. Spray an 8-cup gratin dish with cooking spray.
2. In a large bowl, mix sweet potatoes and nuts. In a small saucepan, melt Earth Balance and add clementine juice and zest, cranberries, spices, and salt. Cook for a few minutes, then stir in soy cream and agave nectar.
3. Stir the liquid into the potato mixture, then spoon into the gratin dish. Sprinkle with nutritional yeast, cover with foil and bake for 35 to 45 minutes or until the gratin is thick and creamy.
4. Remove the foil and drizzle with more agave nectar and bake uncovered for about 5 minutes.

Yield: 6 servings

2 pounds sweet potatoes, peeled and grated (about 6 cups)
½ cup toasted chopped walnuts or pistachios
5 tablespoons Earth Balance
Juice of 3 clementines
Zest of 6 clementines
¾ cup dried cranberries or raisins
¼ teaspoon cinnamon
¼ teaspoon ground cloves
¼ teaspoon ground ginger
4 teaspoons salt, or to taste
¾ cup soy cream (or use soy or nut milk, for a lighter gratin)
½ tablespoon agave nectar or maple syrup (or to taste), plus extra for drizzling
Dash of nutritional yeast

Hint

Instead of hand-grating the sweet potatoes, you can just whiz cut-up chunks of sweet potatoes in the food processor until grainy. A huge timesaver!

KHEER (INDIAN RICE PUDDING)

¼ cup long-grain rice, rinsed

4–5 cups soy or rice milk

1 tablespoon cornstarch

½ cup sugar

2–3 cardamom seeds, crushed

½ teaspoon powdered cardamom

¼ teaspoon salt

3 tablespoons blanched, slivered almonds

3 tablespoons chopped pistachios

2 tablespoons raisins

Kheer is a classic Indian dessert; almost every Indian restaurant I've been to serves it. Happily, you can now enjoy a vegan version. I love the slight heat of the cardamom contrasted against the sticky sweetness of the rice and sugar.

1. Pour rice, milk, cornstarch, sugar, spices, and salt into a medium sauce-pan. Gently bring to a boil, then lower heat and simmer until the rice is soft, about 20 to 25 minutes

2. Add almonds, pistachios, and raisins and simmer for 3 to 4 more min-utes. Pour into a serving dish.

3. Chill for a few hours before serving.

Yield: 4 servings; recipe is easily doubled

GUY FAWKES DAY

Guy Fawkes Day is celebrated in Britain, New Zealand, and in some places in Canada on the evening of November 4. A rather dark holiday, it commemorates the execution of Guy Fawkes for his traitorous role in the Gunpowder Plot of 1605. The actual details of his execution, in keeping with those of the period, are horrific and pretty deplorable. Strangely, the resulting holiday is a lighthearted, jolly affair and involves making a great bonfire and burning an effigy of Guy Fawkes on it. Afterward the crowds enjoy fireworks and, of course, special foods.

MENU: KINDER, GENTLER BONFIRE FARE

LONDON PARTICULAR

This simple, filling soup, combined with the heat of the traditional bonfire, will surely warm you up. It traditionally gets its smokiness from a ham bone, but my version relies on a splash of liquid smoke.

1 cup dried green split peas
2 tablespoons Earth Balance
1 large onion, peeled and diced
3 garlic cloves, minced
1 teaspoon dried thyme
5 cups vegetable or mushroom stock
Freshly ground pepper to taste
Up to 1 teaspoon liquid smoke, or to taste

1. Place the peas in a medium saucepan. Cover with an inch of water and let soak overnight or for at least 8 hours. Drain and rinse.
2. In a stockpot, melt Earth Balance over medium heat. Sauté onion and garlic until soft, about 5 minutes.
3. Add remaining ingredients. Bring to a boil and then cover and simmer until everything is soft, about 1 hour.
4. Carefully puree the soup in the blender in small batches or use an immersion blender. Adjust seasonings and serve.

Yield: 4 servings

Variation

You can make this more colorful by using yellow or red split peas instead of green, but the flavor will essentially be the same. If you are really feeling like channeling your inner domestic god or goddess, you can make half with one color and half with another, and then gently swirl them before serving to achieve a marbled effect. Just be careful not to overswirl, or you will simply have brown pea soup!

INDIAN SHEPHERD'S PIE

Tempeh-Veggie Mixture

1½ tablespoons olive oil

1 large onion, chopped

1 garlic clove, sliced

1 tablespoon garam masala

½ teaspoon turmeric

½ teaspoon ground coriander

¼ teaspoon cayenne pepper (optional)

1 8-ounce package tempeh, crumbled

2 tablespoons lemon juice

Broth made from 1½ cups water and 1 teaspoon miso paste

¾ cup peas (frozen is fine)

2 cups broccoli, cooked and chopped (frozen is fine)

Salt to taste

Mashed Potato Topping

About 1 pound potatoes (4 or 5 potatoes, exact measure is not essential)

2 tablespoons Earth Balance

About ¼–⅓ cup rice or soy milk

½ teaspoon turmeric

½ teaspoon salt, or to taste

Fresh ground pepper, to taste

Instead of going out for curry post–Guy Fawkes festivities, why not try this British-Indian shepherd's pie? It's like a deconstructed samosa, but much healthier, heartier, and prettier—blanketed with gorgeous saffron clouds of mashed potatoes.

1. Grease an 11 x 7-inch baking dish. Preheat oven to 325°F.
2. Heat oil over medium heat in a large skillet. Sauté onion and garlic until soft, about 5 minutes. Add spices and tempeh and stir to coat. Cook about 1 minute.
3. Add lemon juice, broth, and veggies. Bring to a boil. Cover, lower to a simmer, and cook for about 15 minutes, or until most of the liquid is absorbed. Mixture should be slightly wet, and not dry.
4. Meanwhile, if you plan on using a potato ricer, you can leave the skins on; otherwise peel the taters. Cut them into quarters and boil for 10 to 15 minutes or until soft. Mash or rice the potatoes with Earth Balance and enough milk to reach desired consistency. Sprinkle with turmeric and salt and mix well. Adjust seasonings.
5. Pour tempeh mixture into the baking dish. Top with mashed potatoes. Bake for 30 minutes. Let cool for about 5 minutes before serving.

Yield: 4–6 servings

Variations

Substitute cauliflower for broccoli; substitute edamame for peas.

PIMM'S CUP

2 ounces Pimm's No. 1 Cup

1 teaspoon lime juice

Lemon-lime or ginger ale soda

Cucumber slice

Orange slice

This is one of *the* quintessential British cocktails. If you're not the type to do a post-bonfire pub crawl, then consider making a few of these babies at home for you and those in your circle of friends.

Fill a highball glass with ice. Pour in the Pimm's and lime juice, then fill to the top with soda. Garnish with orange and cucumber.

Yield: 1 serving

BARBADOS INDEPENDENCE DAY

Barbados is a little Caribbean island located off the coast of Venezuela that was a British colony from 1627 to November 30, 1966, when the island was granted its independence. Bajans, as residents of Barbados call themselves, celebrate the event with fairs, parades, and of course, special foods. I was lucky enough to be in Barbados one year over Independence Day and got to try some lovely food, so I was very keen to include this chapter.

MENU: BAJAN FLAVORS

TOSTONES

I rarely deep-fry foods, but tostones are one exception. Tostones are a mainstay throughout the Caribbean. These starchy treats are easy and fast to make. They're great on their own, served with a dab of hot sauce. Or you can make them extra large and use them as a base for other foods (like Seitan with Quince, Apple, and Onion on page 46). One of my BFFs, Lisa Larson, taught me to make tostones. She even gave me a tostone press, specially designed for flattening out tostones into a uniform shape. You don't need one, though, as long as you have a spatula.

Canola oil for frying
2 large green plantains (do not use yellow or spotted plantains; they will be too sweet for this dish)
Salt
Hot sauce (optional)

1. Pour about 1 inch of oil in a shallow frying pan. Heat it to medium heat.
2. Peel the plantains, and cut them into ½-inch rounds. (Depending on the thickness of the skin, sometimes, I find it easier to cut them first and then peel.)
3. Fry the plantains in canola oil, about 5 or 6 at a time. Drain well on a paper towel and blot away any excess oil.
4. If you have a tostone press, place a plantain slice in the tostone press chamber and press. If you don't have one, place the tostones on a cutting board and whack them with a spatula to flatten. (This recipe is a great stress reliever!)
5. Fry the squished, flattened rounds again. (Before you admonish me, remember my mantra is "Moderation in all things, including moderation.")
6. Drain on paper towels and sop up as much excess oil as you can.

Yield: 4–6 servings

ISLAND-STYLE TEMPEH

2 8-ounce packages tempeh, each cut into 4 slices or triangles for 8 pieces

1 small pineapple, peeled, cored, and cut into chunks

1–2 teaspoons harissa or your favorite hot sauce

5 cloves garlic

1 cup orange juice

¼ cup lime juice

¾ teaspoon cinnamon

Dash of nutmeg

4 tablespoons chopped fresh cilantro or parsley

½ teaspoon fresh black pepper

1 tablespoon soy sauce

3 tablespoons agave nectar

3 tablespoons olive oil

A little hot, a little sweet, and a little sour thanks to the citrus, this recipe includes all the sunny flavors of the Caribbean. This dish is very filling yet, somehow, very light. Steam the tempeh before baking to remove its inherent bitterness.

1. Steam the tempeh for 5 minutes (see page xi), then drain in a colander. Place in a 9 x 13-inch glass baking dish.
2. Puree all remaining ingredients in a blender until smooth and pour over the tempeh. Cover and marinate overnight or at least 6 hours, turning every now and then.
3. Remove tempeh from marinade. Pour marinade into a saucepan and bring to a boil. Lower to a simmer and cook until the sauce is reduced by half.
4. Heat a grill pan and spray it with cooking spray or add a bit of oil. Cook the tempeh pieces over medium high heat, about 5 to 7 minutes on each side, or until just slightly golden.
5. Transfer to serving plate and drizzle with the sauce.

Yield: 6–8 servings

Variation

Substitute pressed extra-firm tofu or seitan steaks for the tempeh.

CONKIES

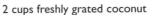

I got my first taste of a *conkie* from a woman in Barbados who was selling them to locals on the street outside my hotel. They were gone within five minutes, and I was lucky enough to have bought one of the prized treats. These mildly sweet cornmeal-based puddings are traditionally steamed in banana leaves, but since I live in the chilly Northeast, we're just going to use aluminum foil (have ready eight 8½ x 8½-inch sheets). Aside from the grating, these are actually quite easy to make. If conkies aren't sweet or moist enough for you, try drizzling a little agave nectar or maple syrup over the top.

1. In a large bowl, mix coconut, pumpkin, and sweet potato.
2. Mix in flour, cornmeal, sugar, raisins, spices, and salt, then add coconut milk, melted Earth Balance, and almond extract. Be sure everything is well combined. Dough will be thick.
3. Place about ½ cup in the middle of each aluminum square sheet. Fold the foil gently around the dough, making sure it is completely sealed. (If water seeps in, it will start to break up the conkie.)
4. Add 1 to 2 inches water to a large pot and bring to a boil; place a steaming rack in pot above the water. Place the foil-wrapped conkies on the rack, cover the pan, and steam until they are firm when poked with a fork, about 45 minutes to 1 hour.
5. Remove the packets from the steamer. Cool for about 15 minutes and keep sealed until serving. Drizzle with extra coconut milk, plus agave nectar or maple syrup, if desired.

Yield: 8 large conkies

2 cups freshly grated coconut
½ cup unsweetened pumpkin puree
1 sweet potato, peeled and grated
½ cup flour
2 cups cornmeal
2 cups packed brown sugar
½ cup raisins
1 teaspoon cinnamon
¼ teaspoon nutmeg
½ teaspoon salt
1 cup coconut milk (light or refrigerated is fine), plus more for drizzling
½ cup (1 stick) Earth Balance, melted
1 teaspoon almond extract
Agave nectar or maple syrup (optional)

MANGO–PASSION FRUIT SORBET

2 cups sugar

2 cups water

1 tablespoon lime juice

Pinch of salt

1 cup passion fruit pulp (I recommend Goya brand)

2 cups mango pulp (again, I recommend Goya brand)

Tart passion fruit contrasted against sweet, fragrant mango. How can you go wrong with this combination? Sorbet is so easy to make. It's refreshing on a hot summer day, and it's a nice change of pace in late fall, as either a palate cleanser between courses or a dessert.

1. In a large saucepan, bring sugar and water to a boil over high heat. Stir in the lime juice and salt, remove from the heat, and let the mixture come to room temperature.
2. Stir in the fruit pulp, then process in an ice-cream maker according to the manufacturer's directions.

Yield: 8 servings

Variation

Pour into molds and make ice pops.

RELIGION-BASED CELEBRATIONS

Organized religion, to me, seems much more divisive than unifying, which is interesting because I doubt anyone would argue that the purest goal of just about every religion (sans politically motivated agendas) is to spread love, goodness, and positivity. When you assess religions objectively, they actually share many more similarities than differences. As Joseph Campbell points out in *The Power of Myth,* the same stories and mythology make fascinating repeat appearances across major religions. The names and settings may be different, but the archetypes and story lines are the same. It's a cliché, but I'll say it anyway: I'm spiritual, but I'm not religious. Still, I love religious celebrations: the rituals, the history, the stories, the food. I want to taste it all. I want to learn from it all.

CANDLEMAS /
LA CHANDALEUR

This is a traditional Catholic feast that celebrates when the Virgin Mary presented the baby Jesus at the temple. But the fact that the French call this holiday "Crepe Day" tells you about the importance of food in this religious holiday.

The French usually eat crepes for breakfast, lunch, and dinner on Candlemas, and they also tell fortunes while making their meals. Each family member holds a coin in one hand, and the crepe pan in the other. Each person tries to flip and catch the crepe in the pan without dropping it. If your reflexes are good and your crepe doesn't hit the floor, it means your family will do well money-wise throughout the year.

MENU: CREPE-A-RAMA

1 cup flour (whole wheat pastry flour is fine)
1¼ cups plain soy milk
½ cup pure water
2 tablespoons soy flour
1 teaspoon vanilla or almond extract (skip this if you're making savory crepes, like Asparagus-Filled Crepes with Blender Hollandaise Sauce, page 94)
¼–½ teaspoon salt
2 tablespoons Earth Balance, melted

BASIC CREPES

This is my basic, go-to crepe recipe. You can fill these crepes with sweet things, like jam, agave nectar, and hazelnut-chocolate spread for breakfast, or fill them with savory treats like sautéed mushrooms, and call them dinner.

Crepes are much easier to make when you use a nonstick pan, but you should not use cooking spray if you use a nonstick pan (it's rumored to ruin the finish); a drop or two of oil will do the trick instead.

1. Whisk all ingredients together in a medium bowl until smooth and no lumps remain. Batter should be thin—add a bit more soy milk, if necessary.
2. Heat sauté or crepe pan over medium-high heat and spray with cooking oil spray. Pour about 3 to 4 tablespoon of batter into pan and immediately twist the pan in one direction so that a thin layer of batter evenly coats the pan.
3. Cook until bottom of crepe is golden. Flip and cook for a few seconds on the other side. Set aside on a plate while you make the rest of the crepes.

Yield: 6 servings

CREPES WITH BANANAS AND GIANDUJA

Banana, hazelnuts, and chocolate are a match made in heaven. Throw them in a crepe and you'll feel like you're sinning. But something this good can't be bad, can it? Gianduja is the generic Italian word for Nutella.

1. For the gianduja, preheat oven to 350°F. Spread nuts on a large cookie sheet and toast until the skins are just about black, about 15 to 20 minutes. Be sure to stir them a few times throughout the toasting process so that everything colors evenly. Remove from oven and let cool.

2. Hazlenut skins are bitter, so they gotta go! Rub the nuts with a tea towel to remove the skins.

3. Process the nuts in a food processor until you have very fine meal (hazelnut flour). Process it as finely as you can. Don't be alarmed if it's a bit sticky. Add the remaining ingredients, and process until smooth, scraping down the sides of the processor as needed. If it's too thick, add more hazelnut oil, 1 tablespoon at a time.

4. To assemble, spread the entire crepe with gianduja. Place banana slices on the bottom half, then gently fold in half, and then in half again. Dust with confectioners' sugar, if you're feeling particularly ambitious. Store excess gianduja in airtight glass jar in the refrigerator—it will keep a few weeks, but it won't last that long.

Yield: 6 servings, plus 1 large jar of leftover gianduja

Gianduja

2 cups raw whole hazelnuts

1 cup confectioners' sugar

⅓ cup Dutch-process cocoa

¼ cup hazelnut oil, plus more, if needed

½ teaspoon vanilla or hazelnut extract, or Tia Maria

¼ teaspoon salt

1 recipe Basic Crepes (see page 92)

2 bananas, thinly sliced on a diagonal

Confectioners' sugar (optional)

ASPARAGUS-FILLED CREPES WITH BLENDER HOLLANDAISE SAUCE

1 recipe Basic Crepes (see page 92)

1 bunch pencil-thin (even anorexic) asparagus, ends trimmed

1 12.3-ounce aseptic box extra-firm silken tofu (do not use refrigerated tofu; it will be too grainy and will not taste right)

6 tablespoons (¾ stick) Earth Balance, melted

¼ teaspoon turmeric (for color)

¼ teaspoon cayenne pepper

½ teaspoon yellow miso thinned with 4 tablespoons lemon juice

Salt to taste

Chopped parsley and sliced scallions for topping

This is one of those dishes that looks like you spent hours preparing, but in reality, it's pretty easy to throw together if you have basic cooking skills. If you're going for the "wow" factor, then this is your recipe.

1. Make crepes and cover them with a hot plate to keep them warm. (You can microwave them to heat them if they get cold.)
2. Bring a large saucepan of water to a boil. Steam asparagus until tender-crisp, about 5 minutes.
3. For the sauce, whiz tofu, Earth Balance, spices, and miso mixture in a blender (or a food processor) until smooth and creamy. Better to overprocess than underprocess. Season to taste with salt and pour into a small saucepan. Turn heat to medium-low and gently heat until warmed through.
4. Put about 3 steamed asparagus spears on the top-front of an open crepe. Loosely roll crepe around asparagus spears. Place on serving plate.
5. Finish each crepe with about 2 tablespoons of the sauce and top with parsley and scallions.

Yield: 6 servings

Variation

Substitute steamed broccoli or sautéed spinach
(with garlic and olive oil) for the asparagus.

VALENTINE'S DAY

Valentine's Day is a time to celebrate love, either by reaffirming your ties with your long-term sweetie or by confessing your attraction to your latest crush. Either way, woo them with this heartbreakingly tasty supper, complete with ingredients that are proven aphrodisiacs.

MENU: INTIMATE DINNER FOR TWO

EASY FRAMBOISE SPRITZER

This pink drink looks elegant, and the berries and liqueur give a sassy boost to dry Cava and Champagne.

Place about 5 raspberries in a champagne flute, and pour in the framboise. Top off with the bubbly.

Yield: 1 serving

Fresh raspberries
2 ounces framboise
6 ounces Champagne, Cava, sparkling Vouvray, or Prosecco

CROSTINI WITH AVOCADO MOUSSE

One of my favorite breakfasts, toast with avocado, inspired this elegant celadon appetizer. It's surprisingly delicious. And easy. Plus avocados are an aphrodisiac, a nice fringe benefit on Valentine's Day (or any day, really).

1. To make crostini, preheat the oven to 375°F. Rub the bread with garlic, then brush with the olive oil. Place on a cookie sheet and bake for 10 minutes, or until golden.
2. To make the mousse, place everything in a food processor and whiz until smooth. Adjust seasonings.
3. Spread mousse on crostini and enjoy.

Yield: 4–6 servings

Crostini
Half loaf good Italian bread, cut into ¾-inch slices
1–2 garlic cloves, peeled and sliced
2 tablespoons olive oil
Salt and pepper to taste

Avocado Mousse
Flesh from 2 ripe avocados
2 teaspoons lemon juice
3 tablespoons vegan sour cream
¼ cup chopped fresh cilantro or parsley
3 tablespoon chopped fresh chives
½ teaspoon sweet paprika
Salt and pepper to taste

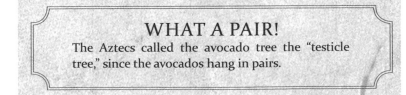

WHAT A PAIR!
The Aztecs called the avocado tree the "testicle tree," since the avocados hang in pairs.

SEITAN WITH PORCINI MUSHROOMS AND SAFFRON

1 cup vegetable broth

¼ cup dried porcini mushrooms

1 pound seitan strips, tenders, or chunks

¼ cup flour

3 tablespoons olive oil

⅓ cup minced shallots

3 garlic cloves, minced

¼ cup dry white wine

⅓ cup chopped fresh parsley

½ teaspoon saffron threads

This is a sexy, sultry dish to make for your sweetie. First, there's something sensual about the earthy mushroom-seitan combination. But the addition of saffron, a powerful aphrodisiac, is the real kicker. The ancient Mediterraneans used saffron in their perfumes, and Cleopatra was reported to have used it in her baths to enhance lovemaking. It seems logical that eating the saffron, rather than applying it topically, will have a more powerful effect.

1. In a medium saucepan, bring the broth to a boil. Add the dried mushrooms and set aside. Mixture needs to soak for about 30 minutes or until mushrooms are soft.
2. Dredge seitan in flour.
3. Heat 2 tablespoons oil in a sauté pan over medium heat. Sauté seitan until brownish, turning as each side browns, about 5 minutes total. Remove from pan.
4. Add the remaining 1 tablespoon oil to the pan along with the shallots and garlic. Sauté until soft, about 5 minutes. Add mushrooms and their soaking liquid, wine, parsley, and saffron. Bring to a boil.
5. Boil until sauce is reduced by half, about 6 minutes. Spoon sauce over seitan and serve over rice, grains, or mashed potatoes.

Yield: 2 servings

CHOCOLATE-COVERED CHERRIES

Anyone can run to the store and buy a heart-shaped box of generic chocolates. But if you make your sweetie these sweeties, he or she will know without a doubt that they are loved. These were my dad's favorite.

1. Drain the jars of cherries and, using paper towels, gently pat dry. (This is very important. Cherries need to be dry. If you have time, let them sit for an hour or two to be extra sure.)
2. Line a large cookie sheet with a Silpat, waxed paper, or parchment paper.
3. In large bowl beat Earth Balance, corn syrup, and salt until smooth. Beat in confectioners' sugar. When it gets too thick to beat, knead by hand until smooth.
4. Shape a 1-inch ball of the dough around each cherry. Place on cookie sheet and set in the freezer until cherries are firm, about 1 hour.
5. Melt chocolate chips and shortening in the microwave in a bowl at 50 percent power. Start with 2 minutes, then stir and continue to nuke in 30-second intervals until the chocolate is melted.
6. Use a fork to dip each cherry into melted chocolate and place on the lined cookie sheet. (If you have leftover chocolate, pour it over the cherries for extra decadence or use it to make some quickie Chocolate-Dipped Things, page 99).
7. Chill until firm and store in the refrigerator.

Yield: 48–52 cherries

2 10-ounce jars maraschino cherries (you need about 50 cherries)

3 tablespoons Earth Balance, softened

3 tablespoons light corn syrup

¼ teaspoon salt

2 cups confectioners' sugar

1 12-ounce package dark chocolate chips

1 tablespoon vegan nonhydrogenated shortening

HEARTFELT LINZER COOKIES

2 cups (4 sticks) Earth Balance, softened

1 cup sugar

1 tablespoon lemon zest

2 teaspoons vanilla

2 cups unbleached white flour

2 tablespoons soy flour

¾ cup ground almonds

1 teaspoon ground cinnamon

¼ teaspoon nutmeg

Pinch cloves

1 cup raspberry jam

About ½ cup confectioners' sugar, for dusting

Nothing says "I love you" better than a batch of these adorably addictive heart-shaped cookies. The slight pucker of the lemon zest and raspberry jam reminds me of the fact that, although love is certainly sweet, a little contrast can liven things up.

1. Preheat oven to 350°F. Spray a cookie sheet with cooking spray or line with Silpat mats.

2. In a medium bowl, cream together the Earth Balance and sugar. Beat in zest and vanilla.

3. In a medium bowl, sift together the flours, almonds, and spices. Stir the dry ingredients into the creamed mixture, about ½ cup at a time. When dough becomes too stiff for a mixer to handle, begin kneading it together with your hands.

4. Lightly flour a large sheet of waxed paper. Roll dough out to ⅛-inch thickness. Cut into heart tops and heart bottoms, using your linzer cookie cutter. (See Think Outside the Cookie Cutter, below.) Place on cookie sheet about 1 inch apart.

5. Bake 9 to 12 minutes or until golden. Cool on wire rack.

6. Dust heart tops with confectioners' sugar.

7. Spread heart bottoms with jam and top with heart tops. (I know this sounds abstract, but follow the directions to the letter and it will all make sense!)

Yield: About 3 dozen, depending on the size of your cookie cutters

Variation

You can substitute any flavor jam for raspberry. Apricot, marmalade, and strawberry work especially well with this recipe.

THINK OUTSIDE THE COOKIE CUTTER

Linzer cookie cutters have interchangeable center shapes, like diamonds, stars, and circles. Using them makes it easy to create professional-looking linzer cookies.

If you don't have linzer cookie cutters (available at most gourmet shops), you can improvise, using two cookie cutters of the same shape (say, hearts, for example). You'll need one big heart and one medium heart.

For the bottom, cut a cookie from one of the larger hearts.

For the top, cut another cookie from the large heart, and then cut out a heart "window" in the center of the cookie, using the smaller heart.

CHOCOLATE-DIPPED THINGS

Chocolate is an aphrodisiac. It's romantic. It contains antioxidants. Blah-blah-blah! We've heard it all before.

Let me cut right to the chase: The real reason I'm sharing this recipe is because it's pathetically easy with an end result so impressive that your sweetie is sure to be touched. Use the best dark chocolate you can get your hands on; it really makes a difference.

1. Line a cookie sheet with waxed paper or a Silpat.
2. Melt the chocolate and shortening in a glass dish in the microwave at 50 percent power, or melt in a double boiler on low heat, until smooth and silky, stirring occasionally.
3. Dip your "things" of choice into the melted chocolate. Gently shake off excess. Place on waxed paper or Silpat. Decorate, if desired. Let harden at room temperature or place in refrigerator to speed up the cool down.

Yield: About 1 cup chocolate dip

1 cup best-quality dark chocolate buttons (I recommend Valrhona)
2 teaspoons nonhydrogenated vegetable shortening

Things to Dip
Apples or apple slices
Brownies
Cherries
Cookies
Cranberries (use a fork to dip)
Crystallized ginger
Dried apricots
Dried banana chips
Frozen bananas
Grapes
Orange slices
Potato chips (yes, potato chips)
Pretzels
Raisins (use a fork to dip)
Strawberries
Vegan graham crackers
Vegan marshmallows
Your favorite unshelled nuts (use a fork to dip)

Optional Decorations
Vegan dusting sugars
Sprinkles
Melted vegan white chocolate for drizzling

St. Patrick's Day

Everyone's Irish on St. Patrick's Day. This celebration began as a Catholic holiday, then became a secular holiday that became a celebration of all things Irish. I say, why stop at wearing green? Why not eat it as well?

MENU: THE EATIN' O' THE GREENS

Colcannon

About 6 large, floury potatoes
(e.g., Russet), scrubbed
(preferably organic)
¾ cup softened Earth Balance
¾–1¼ cups soy or rice milk,
scalded
1 head cabbage, cored and
shredded
1 cup shredded chard (optional)
1 cup tempeh bacon, chopped
1 onion, chopped
¼ cup chopped fresh Italian
parsley
Freshly ground black pepper
Salt to taste

This is classic Irish, rib-sticking food, designed to fill you up and fortify you. It also happens to be simple to throw together.

1. Boil the potatoes in salted water for about 20 minutes or until you can stab them easily with a fork. Drain and rinse with cold water until cool enough to handle.
2. Peel potatoes using a knife and fork, or better yet, put them through a potato ricer into a large bowl.
3. Add Earth Balance and mash with a masher or a fork. Add milk, a bit at a time, stirring continually.
4. Boil the cabbage, and optional chard, in a large pot until tender, about 10 to 15 minutes. Just before draining, toss in the tempeh bacon, cover, and let sit for 5 minutes. Drain well, then add cabbage (and chard) and tempeh bacon, onions, and parsley to mashed potatoes, stirring them in gently.
5. Adjust seasonings and serve.

Yield: 8 servings

CREAM OF BROCCOLI SOUP

Broccoli seems to be abundant and inexpensive all year long, so it's perfect soup fodder. This creamy potage is a snap to prepare. Plus, it's so rich and filling that it's a meal in itself. The hint of nutmeg infuses the broth with a subtle, earthy sweetness.

1. Heat oil in a large stockpot over medium-low heat. Sauté the onion and garlic until translucent, about 5 minutes. Sprinkle salt over onions and garlic.
2. Toss in broccoli. Sauté for 5 or so minutes, until the color intensifies.
3. Add remaining ingredients (except the olive oil and herbs for finishing). Bring to a boil, then lower to a simmer and cook, covered, for 20 to 30 minutes, or until broccoli is soft.
4. Skim off any foam and remove bay leaf. Carefully puree, either using a blender or immersion blender. Make sure all broccoli is totally pulverized.
5. Finish each dish with a drizzle of olive oil and a snippet of fresh herbs if desired.

Yield: 6 servings

2 tablespoons olive oil
2 large onions, chopped
3 garlic cloves, sliced
½–1 teaspoon salt (to taste, if needed)
2 medium heads broccoli, chopped
1 bay leaf
2 cups soy creamer (use soy or rice milk if you are less inclined toward decadence)
2 cups vegetable stock
Pinch of nutmeg
Freshly ground pepper
3 tablespoons nutritional yeast
Best-quality extra-virgin olive oil and fresh herbs (basil, thyme), for finishing (optional)

2 cups soy milk

2 teaspoons vinegar

1 tablespoon baking soda

2 tablespoons sugar

4 cups whole wheat and/or whole grain flour

2 teaspoons salt

1 tablespoon agave nectar

1 tablespoon Earth Balance, melted

IRISH SODA BREAD

The utterly cool thing about Irish Soda Bread is that despite its appearance as an upstanding loaf of bread, absolutely no yeast is required. So this loaf is perfect for the yeast-phobic and the yeast-impaired. It's a hearty dunking bread, great for dipping in the Cream of Broccoli Soup (see page 101) and it also tastes good on its own, slathered with Earth Balance and perhaps a smear of jam if you're eating it for breakfast.

Traditionally, this bread is adorned with a cross. Since Ireland is a Christian country, this symbolism makes perfect sense. But the deep cuts also serve a practical function: they help the bread bake more evenly. If you're not a traditionalist, just carve your initial, a peace sign, or a smiley face instead.

1. Preheat oven to 375°F. Grease a baking sheet or line one with a Silpat.
2. Add vinegar to soy milk. Set aside and let it curdle, about 5 minutes.
3. Sift together dry ingredients. Make a well in the center. Add agave nectar to soy milk and stir. Pour the wet ingredients into the well and mix well, turning out onto a floured board or Silpat. Knead for a minute or two and shape into a round.
4. Place on baking sheet and cut a large cross in the top.
5. Bake for 40 to 45 minutes.
6. Set bread on a wire rack. Brush the top with Earth Balance while it's still warm. Cool for a full hour before slicing.

Yield: 1 loaf

4 tablespoons (½ stick) Earth Balance, softened

4 tablespoons vegan cream cheese

1 teaspoon vanilla

16 ounces confectioners' sugar

2½ cups dried, flaked unsweetened coconut

About 2 tablespoons ground cinnamon, placed in a shallow dish

IRISH POTATOES

Ireland is synonymous with potatoes. These candies are a St. Patrick's Day tradition in the Philadelphia area, whether you are Irish or not. But they don't contain even a smidgen of tater. Their moniker comes from their shape and their "dusty" coating of cinnamon. Put the kids to work, then let them indulge in the fruits—or spuds—of their labor.

1. In a large bowl, cream together the Earth Balance and cream cheese. Add the vanilla, then add the sugar, a bit at a time, until it forms a ball.
2. Stir in the coconut.
3. Using your hands (or your kids' hands!), mold the mixture into 1-inch balls.
4. Roll the "potatoes" in the cinnamon, then place on a cookie sheet.
5. Refrigerate for at least 2 hours or overnight, if you can wait that long.

Yield: About 60 candies

AVOCADO ICE CREAM

I will never forget the St. Patrick's Day when my university cafeteria served green bread. Yes, green. It looked so unappetizing that no one touched it. Fortunately, this lovely celadon soy ice cream gets its lovely hue naturally, thanks to the addition of avocados, which also pump up the richness factor. Warning: This recipe is not for the fat phobic. But then again, fat that comes from coconut and avocados is healthy fat. So relax, and just enjoy already. After all, it's St. Patrick's Day.

1⅔ cups plus ⅓ cup full-fat coconut milk
½ cup plus ¼ cup sugar
1 tablespoon very finely chopped lemon zest
The "guts" of 1 vanilla pod
Pinch of salt
2 tablespoons cornstarch
2 ripe avocados
1 teaspoon lemon juice (to prevent avocado from browning)

1. Heat 1⅔ cups milk, ½ cup sugar, zest, vanilla, and salt over medium heat in a large saucepan.
2. In a small bowl, whisk together ⅓ cup coconut milk, ¼ cup sugar, and cornstarch. Whisk into the heated coconut milk mixture.
3. Bring to a boil, whisking constantly. Boil 1 to 2 minutes. Transfer to a heatproof glass bowl and let cool.
4. Scoop out the avocado flesh and place it in a blender, along with the lemon juice. Add the cooled milk mixture and blend until completely smooth.
5. Transfer to an ice-cream maker and process according to manufacturer's directions.

Yield: 1 quart or 5–6 servings

Mardi Gras

Christians traditionally fast or give up rich or decadent foods during Lent, the forty-day period preceding Easter. Mardi Gras, or Fat Tuesday, is the Tuesday before the fasting begins the following day, on Ash Wednesday. On Mardi Gras, made famous by New Orleans, people tend to "front load" on sweets and other fatty foods, as well as a bit of pre-Lent revelry.

MENU: FEED YOUR FAT TOOTH

Hurricane

1½ cups passion fruit juice

½ cup pineapple juice

½ cup orange juice

1 cup plus 2 tablespoons sugar

¾ cup lime juice

Zest of 1 lime

Splash of bitters

1 cup light rum

1 cup dark rum

3 tablespoons grenadine syrup

6–8 cups ice cubes

Orange slices and maraschino cherries

This is *the* classic Mardi Gras cocktail. It's so famous that it has a glass named after it. Even if you don't serve this "NOLA" libation in an authentic hurricane glass, it will still taste just as sweet.

Mix juices, sugar, zest, bitters, rums, and syrup in a large pitcher until sugar is dissolved. Arrange ice cubes in hurricane glasses (or tall glasses) and pour drink onto the rocks. Adorn with an orange slice and a cherry.

Yield: 8 servings

JAMBALAYA

Jambalaya is classic Louisiana food, built upon the famed "trinity" foundation of flavor: sautéed onion, pepper, and celery. Since you will undoubtedly be drinking on Mardi Gras, this hearty and filling entree will give your stomach a good lining. I don't often add faux meats to my recipes, but the smoky tempeh bacon and sweet-spicy chorizo infuse this dish with some incredible layers of flavor.

1. In a large saucepan, sauté tempeh bacon, onion, pepper, and celery in oil over medium-high heat until fragrant, about 5 minutes.
2. Add garlic, tomatoes, bay leaves, and spices. Stir in rice and slowly add broth.
3. Reduce heat to medium, toss in the vegan sausage and cook until rice absorbs liquid and becomes tender, stirring occasionally, about 25 to 30 minutes. Adjust seasonings. Remove bay leaves, or do as I do: Leave them in and tell whomever gets served the bay leaves that they're good luck.

Yield: 6 servings

1 8-ounce package tempeh bacon, chopped
½ cup chopped onion
½ cup chopped green or red bell pepper, or a combination
½ cup chopped celery
3 tablespoons olive oil
6 garlic cloves, crushed
½ cup chopped tomatoes
2 bay leaves
½ teaspoon paprika
½ teaspoon cayenne pepper
1 teaspoon dried oregano
¾ teaspoon dried thyme
¼ teaspoon salt
¼ teaspoon black pepper
¾ cup white rice*
3 cups vegetable stock
1 cup vegan chorizo or other spicy vegan sausage, crumbled
Salt and pepper to taste

*You can also use brown rice, but you'll need to adjust the cooking time and possibly add more liquid.

Cake

1 cup plus 2 tablespoons soy milk

¼ cup (½ stick) Earth Balance

2 0.25-ounce packages active dry yeast

⅔ cup warm water (110°F)

½ cup packed brown sugar

1½ teaspoons salt

½ teaspoon nutmeg

½ teaspoon ground cardamom

5½ cups unbleached all-purpose flour

2 heaping tablespoons soy flour

Filling

1 cup packed brown sugar

1 tablespoon ground cinnamon

⅔ cup chopped pecans or walnuts (toast them first if you can)

1 teaspoon finely chopped orange or lemon zest

½ cup unbleached all-purpose flour

¼ cup dried chopped figs

¼ cup raisins

½ cup (1 stick) Earth Balance, melted

Glaze

1 cup confectioners' sugar

1 tablespoon water, rum, or brandy

Decorations

Colored sugars

Sprinkles

Food coloring for the glaze

Dragées

Your imagination is the only limit

KING CAKE

A King Cake is a Mardi Gras must, especially if you are from NOLA. It's traditionally decorated with the rainbow colors of a Mardi Gras parade, using sprinkles, food coloring (use natural if you can), and candied fruits. Now I know this next part doesn't exactly sound vegan, but please hear me out: The cake is served with a small baby inside—but it's a plastic baby. Whoever gets the slice with the baby must host the next Mardi Gras party, provided they don't choke on it. (Seriously, please give your guests fair warning about the hidden trinket. And if you're serving this cake to small children, be sure to pre-check the slice for the baby.)

This recipe is time-consuming, but hey, Mardi Gras comes but once a year.

1. To make the cake, scald the soy milk, remove from heat, and stir in Earth Balance. While it's cooling, in a large bowl, dissolve yeast in the warm water with 1 tablespoon of the sugar. Let stand until foamy, about 10 minutes.

2. Stir the cooled soy milk mixture into the yeast mixture. Stir in the remaining sugar, salt, and spices. Then beat in the flour, 1 cup at a time. When you can handle the dough, place it on a lightly floured surface (like a Silpat) and knead until smooth, about 5 minutes. (Or use the bread hook in your mixer, about 3 minutes on medium.)

3. Spray a large bowl with cooking spray and place the dough inside. Spray the top of the dough with cooking spray, then cover with a damp tea towel and let rise in a warm, draft-free place until doubled, about 2 hours.

4. Punch down the dough and divide it in half.

5. Preheat oven to 375°F. Grease two cookie sheets or line with Silpats or parchment.

6. For the filling, combine all ingredients until crumbly.

7. Roll out each dough half into a 6 x 10-inch rectangle. Sprinkle the filling evenly over each half and roll up tightly. Join the ends together to form ring-shaped cakes. Place each on prepared sheets and cut slits evenly across each cake. Let rise in a warm, draft-free place until doubled, about 45 minutes.

8. Bake in the preheated oven for 30 to 35 minutes.

9. Meanwhile, whisk glaze ingredients together in a medium bowl.

10. Remove the cakes from the oven and place the plastic baby in the warm cake. Glaze cake and then decorate to your heart's content.

Yield: 2 King Cakes or about 16 servings

PURIM

Purim is one of the most joyous Jewish celebrations. This holiday centers around Esther, a lovely young woman who was raised by her cousin Mordecai. She was eventually sent to the King of Persia to become part of his harem. The king grew to love Esther much more than any of the other women in the harem, and eventually he made her queen. But since she had sworn to her faithful cousin never to reveal the details of her identity, the king did not know she was Jewish.

Haman, one of the king's advisors, planned to exterminate all Jews. At this point, Mordecai asked Esther to speak to the king on behalf of her people. She fasted for three days beforehand to mentally prepare herself. She told the king, and also told him of Haman's plot, thus saving the Jewish people. Haman and his ten sons were hanged.

Today, people celebrate Purim by first embarking on a fast, then they enjoy a feast of food and drink, give gifts of food and drink, and donate to charity. In modern celebrations, children also dress up in costumes.

MENU: ESTHER'S TABLE

ESTHER'S BAKED FALAFEL

While Esther lived with the King of Persia, she ate mainly beans and peas in order to stay kosher, which is why you traditionally eat chickpeas on Purim—and why every vegan chick has a secret girl crush on Esther.

Now all vegan girls love their falafel. But fried foods are not great for your health, which is why I'm including this recipe for Baked Falafel. Besides being healthier, it's also much easier to make. Plus, frying is just messy. Serve these little balls of happiness with the accompanying Smoky Tahini Sauce (see page 108) in a pita, stuffed with fresh veggies, or atop rice or whole grains.

2 tablespoons olive oil
1 15-ounce can chickpeas, rinsed and drained
½ small onion, minced
3 garlic cloves, minced
2 tablespoons chopped fresh parsley
2 tablespoons flour, plus more if needed
1½ teaspoons cumin
½ teaspoon coriander
½ teaspoon baking powder
¼ teaspoon black pepper
Salt to taste

1. Preheat oven to 350°F. Drizzle oil on a high-sided cookie sheet or in a baking pan.
2. Place remaining ingredients in food processor and whiz until it forms a dough. You may need to remove the dough with your hands and work it a bit. If the dough is not sticking to itself, add flour, a teaspoon at a time, until it does.
3. Form into 2-inch balls or patties. Place in the oiled pan.
4. Bake for 10 to 12 minutes on one side, or until golden. Flip and bake on the other side another 10 to 12 minutes, or until golden. Drain on paper towels.

Yield: 4 servings

½ cup tahini

2 garlic cloves, minced

⅓ cup lemon juice (approximately 2 lemons)

½ teaspoon salt

1 teaspoon smoked paprika

½ teaspoon sumac (a lemony Middle Eastern herb)

⅓ cup water

2 tablespoons chopped fresh cilantro

SMOKY TAHINI SAUCE

It's the perfect topping for Esther's Baked Falafel (see page 107), but it also perks up salads, whole grains, and steamed veggies.

Combine everything in a blender and whiz until smooth.

Yield: About ¾ cup

Variation

To make this a dip instead of a sauce, reduce the water to 2 tablespoons.

1 cup sugar

½ cup (1 stick) Earth Balance, softened

¼ cup oil

3 tablespoons lemon juice

1 tablespoon orange or lemon zest

1 teaspoon vanilla

¼ cup soy or rice milk

2–2¾ cups flour

¼ cup soy flour

1 tablespoon baking powder

1 cup apricot, raspberry, or strawberry jam, or 1 cup mincemeat

HAMANTASCHEN

Hamantaschen (Haman's hats) are named after the infamous Haman, the villain of Purim who intended to exterminate the Jews. Unlike Haman, these little triangle cookies are famously sweet. There are as many Hamantaschen fillings as there are Jewish *bubbies*. But in the spirit of keeping things simple, we're using jams and mincemeat. But please, feel free to use your own *bubby's* filling recipe.

1. Spray two cookie sheets with cooking spray or line with Silpats.
2. Cream together the sugar and Earth Balance. Add oil, lemon juice and zest, and vanilla. Add enough milk to form a workable dough; this totally will depend on the humidity in your city. Philadelphia is so humid that I don't have to add any, but if you live in a drier city, you may need to add even more.
3. Add dry ingredients and beat until smooth.
4. Refrigerate for 1 hour.
5. Preheat oven to 350°F.
6. Divide dough into 3 or 4 sections. Take out 1 section of dough and roll out to ⅛-inch thickness. Cut into 3-inch-ish circles using a glass or cookie cutter. Place 1 teaspoon of jam or filling in the middle of each circle.
7. To form each cookie, fold 3 sides of the circle over the filling, leaving the middle open. Pinch the 3 corners so the dough sticks together and forms a triangle.
8. Bake for 18 to 20 minutes. Cool on a rack.

Yield: 24–28 cookies

SESAME SEED COOKIES

Traditionally you eat seeds and foods with seeds on Purim because, as the story goes, Esther ate seeds (and beans) while in the temple so as to avoid eating nonkosher food. These cookies are crispy and not overly sweet, perfect for dipping in tea.

1. Preheat oven to 350°F. Grease a cookie sheet or line with Silpat.
2. Cream together sugar, Earth Balance, vanilla, and rice milk.
3. Sift together flours and baking soda. Add to the creamed mixture, a few tablespoons at a time, and mix until smooth. Stir in the sesame seeds.
4. Roll into small walnut-size balls. Place each ball on the greased cookie sheet, pressing each cookie down with your thumb. Bake for about 20 minutes or until golden.

Yield: 22–28 cookies

½ cup sugar

5 tablespoons Earth Balance, softened

1 teaspoon vanilla

1 tablespoon rice milk

½ teaspoon baking soda

½ cup flour

2 tablespoons soy flour

¼ teaspoon salt

2 cups sesame seeds

EASTER

For Christians around the world, Easter is a holiday that celebrates rebirth and renewal. Children look forward to Easter egg hunts and to the chocolates and treats that the Easter Bunny leaves them. Happily, these days many Easter egg hunts rely on colorful plastic eggs, and are therefore both vegan and chicken friendly.

MENU: EASTER BUNNY BREAKFAST

SUMMER SQUASH AND APPLESAUCE MUFFINS

2 cups shredded summer squash (yellow squash or yellow zucchini)

2 cups sugar

¼ cup soy flour

½ cup canola oil

¼ cup unsweetened applesauce

1 tablespoon vanilla

3 cups flour (I use half spelt and half whole wheat pastry flour)

1½ tablespoons baking powder

1 teaspoon baking soda

2 teaspoons cinnamon

1 teaspoon salt

½ cup raisins (optional)

½ cup chopped walnuts (optional)

You know that when the Easter Bunny visits, the kids are going to be all sugared out. Before church and the egg hunts, start them off with these semi-healthy muffins. And thanks to the squash and whole grain flours, you can rest assured that the kids will be ingesting at least *some* fiber, phytochemicals, and vitamins. They freeze beautifully, too.

1. Preheat oven to 350°F. Line muffin tins with paper cups, or spray them lightly with cooking spray.
2. Place shredded squash in a colander to drain for at least 30 minutes. Just before using, squeeze out any excess moisture.
3. In a large bowl, mix drained squash, sugar, soy flour, canola oil, applesauce, and vanilla until moistened. Add remaining dry ingredients and mix until just blended. (Do not overmix or you will end up with tough muffins!) Fold in nuts and raisins, if using.
4. Fill muffin tins ⅔ full with batter and bake for 18 to 24 minutes, or until knife, cake tester, or toothpick inserted in center comes out clean. Tops should be golden brown. Allow to cool fully on a rack before eating.

Yield: 18 muffins

CHOCOLATE–PEANUT BUTTER EASTER EGGS

These were a classic growing up, so I veganized my mom's recipe by substituting Earth Balance for butter, and shortening for paraffin (gasp! I can't believe we ate it). My mom made them just about every year, and they were devoured in no time flat.

1. In a large mixing bowl, combine confectioners' sugar, peanut butter, and Earth Balance. The mixture will be extremely thick. (Depending on the moisture level in your climate, the mixture may be too thick to mix. If this is the case, add a tablespoon or so of soy or rice milk.) Knead with your hands or a mixer's dough hook until everything is mixed in. Refrigerate dough for a few hours or overnight.
2. Depending on how many eggs you want to make, line a cookie sheet or two with waxed paper, parchment paper, or a Silpat.
3. In a medium saucepan, melt chocolate and shortening together over medium heat. Using a fork (or tongs, if you are making just 2 large eggs), dip an egg in the melted chocolate to cover and then set on waxed paper.
4. Put eggs in the refrigerator to facilitate hardening the chocolate.
5. Decorate the eggs with frosting, if desired.

Yield: 2–25 eggs, depending on desired size

1 16-ounce package confectioners' sugar
1 cup creamy all-natural peanut butter
3 tablespoons Earth Balance
1 tablespoon nonhydrogenated vegan shortening
¾ cup dark chocolate chips or buttons
Frosting for decoration (optional)

1 8-ounce container nonhydrogenated vegan cream cheese, at room temperature

4 cups confectioners' sugar

½ teaspoon vanilla

Pinch of salt

1 tablespoon Earth Balance, softened

1 cup shredded coconut (sweetened or not, depending on your taste; I prefer unsweetened)

1 tablespoon nonhydrogenated vegan shortening

2 cups dark chocolate chips or buttons

Frosting for decoration (optional)

COCONUT-CREAM EASTER EGGS

Another one of my mom's classic Easter treats, veganized.

1. Depending on how many eggs you want to make, line a cookie sheet or two with waxed paper, parchment paper, or a Silpat.

2. In a large mixing bowl, beat together cream cheese, confectioners' sugar, vanilla, coconut, and Earth Balance. Mixture should be extremely thick. (Depending on the moisture level in your climate, the mixture may be too thick to mix. If this is the case, add a tablespoon or so of soy or rice milk.) Knead with your hands or a mixer's dough hook until everything is mixed in. Form into egg shapes, place on a tray and freeze dough for a few hours or overnight.

3. In a medium saucepan, melt chocolate and shortening together over medium heat. Using a fork (or tongs, if you are making just 2 large eggs), dip an egg in the melted chocolate to cover then set on waxed paper.

4. Put eggs in the refrigerator to facilitate hardening the chocolate.

5. Decorate the eggs with frosting, if desired.

Yield: 2–25 eggs, depending on desired size

HOT CROSS BUNS

These subtly sweet buns are traditionally eaten during Easter time, more specifically, on Good Friday, the day that commemorates the crucifixion of Christ, hence their name. Hot Cross Buns are a treat for breakfast, slightly warmed, slathered with Earth Balance, and washed down with a cup of Earl Grey tea.

1. Soak the currants and raisins in about 2½ cups of water for at least 20 minutes. Drain very well.
2. Pour warm water into a large mixing bowl. Sprinkle yeast and 1 teaspoon of the sugar over the water. Let it sit until foamy, about 5 minutes.
3. Add to the bowl the remaining sugar, salt, flours, and spices (about 1 cup at a time). Mix until combined, scraping down the sides as needed. Add Earth Balance. Switch to a dough hook, or knead manually when dough becomes too thick for the mixer to handle. Mix in currants and raisins by hand using a heavy spatula. Cover with a damp tea towel or plastic wrap and let rest about 1 hour.
4. Punch dough down on a floured surface, such as waxed paper or a Silpat. Cover and let rest 10 more minutes.
5. Preheat oven to 375°F.
6. Shape dough into 12 balls and place them on a large, greased cookie sheet. Again, cover and let rise in a warm place till doubled, about 40 minutes.
7. Gently brush canola oil on balls.
8. Bake for about 15 minutes or until golden. Cool completely on a wire rack.
9. Meanwhile, make glaze by whisking together all glaze ingredients.
10. Brush an X onto each cooled bun with glaze. Or if you really want to get fancy, pipe on Xs using a pastry bag.

Yield: 12 buns

½ cup dried currants
⅓ cup raisins
¾ cup warm water (110°F)
1 tablespoon active dry yeast
¼ cup plus 1 teaspoon sugar
½ teaspoon salt
3 cups unbleached all-purpose flour
2 heaping tablespoons soy flour
3 tablespoons Earth Balance, softened
1 teaspoon ground cinnamon
¼ teaspoon nutmeg
Pinch of turmeric (for color)
1 tablespoon canola oil

Glaze
½ cup confectioners' sugar
¼ teaspoon vanilla extract
1 teaspoon finely grated lemon zest
2 teaspoons soy, rice, hemp, or coconut milk

PASSOVER

This important religious holiday celebrates the exodus and eventual emancipation of the Jews from slavery in Egypt. Families enjoy a myriad of traditional foods during the Seder dinner. Traditionally a lamb was symbolically slaughtered. Today, veggie Jews enjoy kinder, gentler, and healthier feasts.

MENU: PASSOVER SEDER

BAKED AGAVE TOFU OR TEMPEH

1 pound extra-firm tofu or 2
  8-ounce packages tempeh
¼ cup lemon or orange juice
1 teaspoon fresh ground ginger
1½ teaspoons soy sauce
⅓ cup agave nectar
½ teaspoon cinnamon
2 tablespoons olive oil
Pepper to taste

This is an easy, kid-friendly Passover dish: Just press, mix, and bake. To make it more kid friendly, cut the protein into even smaller pieces.

1. If using tofu, press it first (see instructions on page xi), then cut it into 4 triangles. If using tempeh, cut into 4 triangles and steam for 10 minutes (see page xi).
2. Whisk together remaining ingredients in a shallow baking dish.
3. Marinate your protein of choice for at least 6 hours, or preferably overnight.
4. Preheat oven to 350°F. Bake for about 1 hour, flipping now and then and basting occasionally with marinade.

Yield: 4 servings, recipe is easily doubled or tripled

Variation

Substitute 4 large seitan steaks or 1 pound of seitan chunks for the tofu or tempeh.

HAROSETH

Haroseth is a standby on the Passover table. This sweet paste symbolizes the bricks and mortars that the children of Israel made while they were enslaved in Egypt. You can eat haroseth spread on matzo, as a dressing (add a bit of water to thin out), or as a condiment. Try a bit with the Baked Agave Tofu or Tempeh (page 114).

Mix everything in the food processor until it forms a thick paste. If mixture is too thick, add some additional water or agave nectar, 1 tablespoon at a time.

Yield: 1 healthy cup

1 cup unsalted pistachios
½ cup unsalted walnuts
¼ cup pitted dates
¼ cup pitted prunes
¼ cup dried apricots
1 tart apple (like Granny Smith), peeled, cored, and quartered
¼ cup pomegranate juice
¼ cup sweet Passover wine
2 tablespoons agave nectar
1 teaspoon lemon juice
1 teaspoon finely grated lemon zest
½ teaspoon cinnamon
⅛ teaspoon nutmeg
Pinch of salt

POTATO KUGEL

Potato kugel is classic comfort food. How can you go wrong with the potato-onion-salt combo? The addition of nutritional yeast infuses the potatoes with a slightly cheesy, creamy flavor.

1. Preheat oven to 375°F. Pour half the oil into a 9 x 13-inch baking pan.
2. In a large bowl, mix remaining ingredients, including the rest of the oil.
3. Place the pan with oil in the heated oven for about 5 minutes. Heating the pan and oil will help give your kugel a crispy, golden crust.
4. Pour the batter into the pan and bake for about 1 hour, or until the top is golden. Let cool for about 10 minutes before serving.

Yield: 6 servings

6 tablespoons olive oil, divided
6 large potatoes, peeled and shredded
1 large onion, finely chopped
1 teaspoon salt
Freshly ground pepper to taste
½ cup nutritional yeast
6 tablespoons chopped fresh parsley

Variation

Substitute yams or sweet potatoes for the potatoes
and add 1 teaspoon cinnamon.

6 tablespoons Earth Balance

½ cup packed brown sugar

½ teaspoon vanilla

4 sheets matzo

½ cup best-quality dark chocolate buttons or chips

½ teaspoon salt

⅓ cup crushed nuts (optional)

CHOCOLATE-COVERED MATZO

When the Jews fled Egypt, they had to leave so quickly that they didn't have time to allow their bread to rise. And so matzo was born.

Matzo is rather austere by its nature, but with all the chocolate and sugar in this recipe, you won't miss the yeast one bit! Served in a pretty tin container, a batch of Chocolate-Covered Matzo also makes a great host or hostess gift.

1. Preheat oven to 400°F. Line 2 baking sheets with aluminum foil or Silpat mats.
2. In a small saucepan, melt together the Earth Balance, brown sugar, and vanilla.
3. Place two matzos on each baking sheet. Using a spatula, spread the sugar mixture thinly over the top of the matzo. Don't worry about being perfect; just try to cover as much as you can.
4. Bake matzos for 5 to 6 minutes or until the topping is bubbly and brown.
5. Remove from the oven and immediately sprinkle each hot matzo with chocolate. Cover with another baking pan to seal in heat (without touching the chocolate) and let sit for about 1 minute. Use a spatula or icing knife to spread chocolate evenly over the matzos. Sprinkle with nuts, if desired, and press nuts gently into melted chocolate.
6. Place in refrigerator or freezer to cool. Break into pieces and store in an airtight container.
7. If you prefer an artier matzo, you can melt the chocolate and use a spatula to swirl it atop the matzo, Jackson Pollack–style. If you choose this route, I recommend skipping the nuts.

Yield: About 2 dozen pieces

HANUKKAH

Hanukkah celebrates the Jewish Maccabees' military victory over the Greek-Syrians and their recapture of an important temple. It is spread out over eight nights, and one candle on the menorah is lit each night to symbolize the fact that the oil lamps in the temple burned for eight days. Children get a small gift each night of this important holiday. Families traditionally share meals, play games, and eat oil-heavy food to commemorate the oil.

MENU: HANUKKAH SUPPER

MEGA-ISRAELI SALAD

Chop-chop! That's the hardest part about making this salad. Besides the traditional onion, cucumber, tomato, and pepper mixture, I've added a few more veggies like avocado and corn (if only because it was one less thing to chop). I love the straightforward, Mediterranean flavor of the lemony dressing. I created this recipe for Hanukkah, but this salad is exceptionally refreshing on a hot summer day. It's best eaten right after making it.

1. In a large bowl, combine all vegetables and parsley. Sprinkle with olive oil and toss.
2. Add lemon juice, adjust seasonings, and toss again.

Yield: 6 servings

3 tomatoes, seeded and chopped
1 seedless cucumber, peeled and chopped
1 green pepper, seeded and chopped
1 red pepper, seeded and chopped
1 avocado, halved, flesh scooped out and diced
1 red onion, chopped
½ cup cooked corn
¼ cup chopped fresh parsley
1 garlic clove, minced
2 tablespoons olive oil
Juice of 1 lemon (about 3 tablespoons)
½ teaspoon salt
¼ teaspoon pepper

About 3 pounds potatoes, peeled
  and grated
4 garlic gloves, minced
1 onion, grated
¼ cup silken aseptic tofu
  (I recommend Mori Nu)
½ teaspoon baking powder
1 teaspoon salt
½ teaspoon pepper
3 tablespoons flour
Canola oil for frying

UPDATED LATKES

When the Second Temple of Israel was being rededicated, there was only enough oil to burn the menorah for one night. Amazingly, the flames burned on for eight nights. Latkes are a popular Hanukkah food since they are fried in oil, a nod to the story of the miracle flame. They are also popular because they taste terrific. Everyone loves them!

These are one of the few fried foods that I make regularly, probably because I grew up with potato pancakes and consider them comfort food. Although I was not raised Jewish, my Polish *babci* (grandma) used to make these once a week. We called them "bleenies." Whatever you call them, they are damn tasty, especially topped with a dollop of applesauce or dairy-free sour cream.

1. In a large bowl, mix together all ingredients except for canola oil.
2. In a large frying pan, over medium heat, heat a few tablespoons of oil. Drop batter onto pan and flatten to form latkes. You can cook about 3 at a time in a large pan.
3. Cook until golden, then flip and cook the other side for a few seconds. Drain and cool on paper towels.

Yield: 6–8 servings

Variations

Mix in about ⅓ cup Daiya cheese to the batter
Substitute sweet potatoes for the potatoes.
Add about ½ cup matzo meal to the batter.

INSANELY THICK AND COMFORTING SQUASH SOUP

This ridiculously thick and creamy soup, served with plenty of bread for dunking, gives you an instant reprieve from the cold. It's like a hug in a bowl. It's the perfect start to a Hanukkah supper. Did I mention that it takes about seven minutes of hands-on time?

1. Place all ingredients in a large saucepan. Start with just 1 cup of vegetable broth and add more later if you prefer a thinner soup. Break up the tofu with your spatula. Don't worry if it looks a bit wonky; you'll puree it after cooking.
2. Bring to a boil and then lower heat to medium. Cook, partially covered, for 30 minutes, or until squash and potatoes are soft. Add more broth, if needed.
3. Process with an immersion blender until completely smooth. Drizzle each serving with extra-virgin olive oil—for flavor, color contrast, and a bit of tradition!

Yield: 4 servings

12 ounces frozen cooked winter squash (or 1½ cups cubed fresh winter squash)

12.3-ounce aseptic container fat-free, firm tofu (do not use refrigerated tofu; the texture will be too grainy]

3 small organic potatoes, cut into sixths (no peeling required)

½ small onion, roughly chopped

3–5 cloves garlic, sliced

1–1½ cups vegetable broth

3 tablespoons nutritional yeast

1 bay leaf

1 teaspoon dry sage

Dash of nutmeg

½ teaspoon salt, or to taste

Freshly ground black pepper

Extra-virgin olive oil for drizzling

Serving Suggestion
Top with Candied Squash Seeds (see page 76).

RUE DES ROSIERS PAIN D'ÉPICES

1½ cups almond or soy milk

⅔ cup agave nectar

¼ cup molasses

1 teaspoon vanilla

¼ cup canola oil

2 cups flour

¼ cup soy flour

1 tablespoon baking powder

1 teaspoon baking soda

¼ teaspoon salt

¾ teaspoon cinnamon

½ teaspoon ground ginger

½ teaspoon nutmeg

¼ teaspoon cloves

This quick bread traditionally shows up in bakeries throughout France in the weeks before Christmas, but to me, it seems more like a Hanukkah sweet, which is why I've named it after the Rue des Rosiers, a popular street in one of Paris's Jewish neighborhoods, best known for its falafel restaurants. I love this spice bread for breakfast, slathered with Earth Balance and marmalade, along with a cup of hot mulled tea or cider.

1. Preheat oven to 350°F. Grease a 9 x 5-inch loaf pan or four mini loaf pans.
2. In a medium bowl, whisk together the wet ingredients.
3. In a large bowl, sift together the dry ingredients. Make a well in the center and add the wet ingredients, stirring until just combined. Do not overstir.
4. Pour the batter in the prepared pan and bake for 45 to 55 minutes, or until a cake tester inserted in the middle comes out clean. (Bake 20 to 24 minutes for mini loaves.)

Yield: 1 large or 4 mini loaves

Variations

Add ½ cup of any of the following, or a combination:

Dried cranberries

Raisins

Chopped dates

Chopped dried figs

Toasted walnuts, pecans, or almonds

Candied ginger

Chocolate or carob chips

SUFGANIYOT

Hanukkah wouldn't be the same without these tasty jelly-filled doughnuts. As is the case with most Jewish food, there is a symbolism attached to their yumminess: Like latkes, the oil they are fried in symbolizes the oil lamps that burned for eight days in the story of Hanukkah.

1. In a small bowl, stir together the yeast, teaspoon of sugar, and warm water until dissolved. Let it sit for about 5 to 10 minutes, or until the mixture begins to froth.
2. In a large bowl, sift together the ⅓ cup sugar, flour, cinnamon, and salt. Stir in the soy milk, Earth Balance, and vanilla. Add the yeast mixture, a bit at a time, and stir until a stiff dough forms. Cover with foil or a damp tea towel and allow to sit for 1 hour in a warm place.
3. Knead the dough on a floured surface or Silpat until smooth, just a minute or two, then roll out to about ¾-inch thickness. Once again, cover with a damp tea towel and let rise for about 20 minutes, until doubled in size. Use a doughnut cutter or glass (about 3-inch diameter) to cut out round shapes. Place about 1 teaspoon of jam in the center and fold dough over, forming as round a shape as possible.
4. Heat a few inches of oil over medium-high in a deep pan, being very, very careful not to splash it (I suggest you wear a long-sleeved, tight-fitting top). Place a scrap of dough in the oil. If it rises almost immediately, the oil is ready.
5. Fry the doughnuts until golden on both sides, turning as needed. Only fry 2 or 3 at a time; don't crowd the pan. Drain on paper towels. Let cool.
6. Place the confectioners' sugar in a brown paper bag. Add a few cooled doughnuts at a time and gently shake the bag to coat the doughnuts with confectioners' sugar.

Yield: About 12 doughnuts

2 0.25-ounce packages yeast (about 1½ tablespoons)
⅓ cup plus 1 teaspoon sugar
1 cup warm water (110°F)
4 cups whole wheat pastry flour
Pinch of cinnamon
½ teaspoon salt
1 cup soy milk
¼ cup (½ stick) Earth Balance, melted
1 teaspoon vanilla
About 1 cup grape, strawberry, or apricot jam (or your favorite)
Canola oil for frying
About 1 cup confectioners' sugar

CHRISTMAS EVE

On Christmas Eve, many families of European descent gather for the feast of the seven fishes, a meal in which seven different fish-based foods are served. A modern, kinder version of this tradition includes seven different grain-based dishes from different cultures. Plus, there's no nasty mercury involved.

MENU: FEAST OF THE SEVEN GRAINS

1–2 tablespoons rice vinegar
2 cups cooked brown rice, fluffed with a fork, at room temperature
4 nori sheets
1 ripe avocado, sliced (prepare the avocado just before assembling sushi or it will turn brown)
½ cup oil-packed sun-dried tomatoes, drained (if you're fat phobic you can use dried tomatoes, reconstituted in water)
Pickled ginger, wasabi, and soy sauce for serving

Variation

You can use other vegetables in the sushi roll: whole scallion, asparagus, or cucumber strips, for example.

BROWN RICE CHRISTMAS MAKI

Sushi for Christmas? Why not? These rolls are even red and green—perfectly Santa appropriate.

Don't be upset if you are a sushi newbie and you have to sacrifice your first roll to the sushi gods. Go easy on yourself: Sushi masters weren't made in a day. These still taste great, even if you are not the best sushi roller. Careful—once you get the hang of making sushi, it's addictive.

1. Stir the rice vinegar into the rice. Keep stirring until it becomes st licky, almost like rice "dough." The amount of vinegar you need will vary depending on where you live, how dry the rice is, and so on. Try not to fret too much about it; as long as it's sticky, you should be fine. Let the rice cool completely to room temperature.
2. Lay a sheet of nori on a bamboo sushi mat (or on a piece of waxed paper if you're a sushi newbie).
3. Spread rice over the nori sheet, leaving a ½-inch of nori uncovered at the top.
4. Place a slender strip of avocado close to the bottom of the the nori sheet horizontally. Next to it, as close as possible, place a slender strip of sun-dried tomato. If using more veggies, add them, keeping them as close to their neighbors as possible.
5. Here comes the fun part: roll! Start at the bottom edge nearest you and slowly and methodically roll toward the uncovered edge, using your bamboo mat (or waxed paper) to help press everything together tightly. Seal the uncovered edge with a tiny bit of water and set the roll aside for at least 10 minutes.
6. With a very sharp, serrated knife, cut the roll into 6 to 8 pieces. Serve with pickled ginger, wasabi, and soy sauce.

Yield: 4 servings

POLENTA-KALE CUTLETS WITH BASIL AIOLI

$

Who doesn't love to eat a good cutlet? This is an easy, nontraditional way to prepare polenta—and a surreptitious tactic to get the little ones (and finicky adults) to eat their greens. With a nod to the season, the slightly sweet Basil Aioli is a highbrow and festive complement to the kale's slight bitterness, but happily the cutlets pair just as nicely with pantry staple sauces like ketchup and barbecue sauce.

1. To prepare the greens, heat 1 tablespoon oil in a large nonstick sauté pan. Sauté the garlic and red pepper flakes over medium-low heat until garlic is translucent, taking great care not to burn. Add kale (or other greens) and cook until soft, 20 to 30 minutes (5 to 10 minutes for spinach or chard). Add water or broth as needed to help steam-cook the veggies. Set aside.
2. To prepare the polenta cutlets, mix greens, milk, broth, and salt in a large saucepan, Bring to a boil. Whisk in cornmeal, a bit at a time, taking care that no lumps form. Turn heat to low and whisk continually until the mixture is extremely thick. Switch to a wooden spoon when the whisk becomes unmanageable. Stir until virtually all of the excess moisture evaporates, about 20 to 30 minutes. Pour into a 9 x 13-inch greased pan and refrigerate for at least 30 minutes or overnight. This will make it easier to form into cutlets. Score into 10 or 12 even sections.
3. To prepare the aioli, mix all ingredients in a food processor until smooth. Set aside if you'll eat after frying the polenta or refrigerate and bring to room temp to serve.
4. After the polenta has set, heat some oil over medium-high heat in a large frying pan. Remove 2 polenta squares. Place them in pan and using a spatula, lightly tap them down into a cutlet shape. Fry until golden brown, about 5 to 10 minutes, then carefully flip and cook the other side about 5 to 10 minutes. Repeat with the remaining polenta. Serve immediately with Basil Aioli or the sauce of your choice (see Variations below).

Yield: 6–8 servings

Polenta Cutlets

1 tablespoon olive oil, plus oil or cooking spray for frying cutlets
3 garlic cloves, minced
¼–½ teaspoon red pepper flakes
1 large bunch kale, trimmed and finely chopped—about 3 cups (you may substitute spinach, collard greens, or chard; frozen, thawed, and drained is fine, too)
2–3 tablespoons water or vegetable broth
1 cup soy or rice milk
3 cups veggie broth or water
½ teaspoon salt
1 cup cornmeal

Basil Aioli

½ cup Vegenaise
2 garlic cloves
1 slice bread, crumbled
3 tablespoons coarsely chopped fresh basil
Salt and pepper to taste

Variations

Serve with your favorite sauce or veggie-centric toppings:

Pesto
Yogurt-Tahini Sauce (see page 137)
Mushrooms and your favorite herbs sautéed in oil and white wine
Caramelized onions
Teriyaki sauce
Your favorite barbecue sauce
Cumin-Harissa Dipping Sauce (see page 166)

GUSSIED-UP TABBOULEH

1 cup dry bulgur

1½ cups vegetable broth

Small punch Italian parsley, chopped (about 1 cup)

Small bunch mint, chopped (about 1 cup)

3 cloves garlic, minced

2–3 tomatoes, chopped

1 small onion or 1 small bunch scallions, finely chopped

⅓ cup grated carrot or carrot pulp leftover from juicing (optional)

Juice and zest of 1 small organic lemon

4 tablespoons extra-virgin olive oil

Salt and pepper to taste

Optional additions: finely chopped black olives, capers, raisins, toasted pine nuts or sunflower seeds

Although tabbouleh is not typical Christmas fare, it's one of those dishes that everyone seems to like. When I first became vegetarian, it was one of the few dishes in my culinary repertoire. I updated this Middle Eastern staple, which showcases sassy fresh herbs against sweet and chewy bulgur. I added a bit of lemon zest to brighten the flavors and further enhance the dish's inherent freshness. And instead of soaking the bulgur in water, I soak it in veggie broth for an added layer of flavor.

1. In a medium bowl, soak the bulgur in the broth for 30 minutes.
2. Mix the remaining ingredients together in a large bowl.
3. Stir the plumped bulgur into the ingredients in the large bowl. Chill or serve at room temperature.

Yield: 8 servings

Variation

Use orange, Mandarin orange, clementine, or tangerine juice and zest instead of lemon.

GOLDEN MILLET PILAF

This gorgeous saffron-hued pilaf makes an elegant side dish that just so happens to be gluten-free. Top it with the Pan-Seared Tofu with Basil-Balsamic Glaze (see page 153) or the Island-Style Tempeh (see page 88). It's also a wonderful base for the Millet-Stuffed Mushrooms with Aioli (see page 78).

1. Bring the broth to a boil in a large saucepan.
2. Add remaining ingredients. Lower heat, cover, and simmer for about 25 to 30 minutes, or until you can fluff up millet with a fork. Adjust seasonings.

Yield: 6 servings as a side

2½ cups vegetable broth
1 cup millet
1 tablespoon extra-virgin olive oil
4 garlic cloves, crushed
6 green onions, sliced
½ cup pitted and chopped green olives
1½ cups chopped organic spinach
1 tablespoon dried basil
2 teaspoons dried oregano
4 tablespoons chopped fresh parsley
½ teaspoon turmeric (for color)
½ teaspoon salt, or to taste
Freshly ground pepper to taste

THE DIRTY DOZEN

Although I would love to buy organic everything, I would quickly go broke if I did. Organic produce prices are coming down, slowly but surely, thanks to increased demand that creates increased supply, but still, most people can't afford to go 100 percent organic. The "Dirty Dozen" is the Environmental Working Group's list of the twelve most pesticide-laden crops. I always buy the Dirty Dozen organic, and other items when prices are reasonable. Get the current list at www.foodnews.org, and check back from time to time, because the list changes often.

CARIBBEAN WHEAT BERRY SALAD

1½ cups uncooked wheat berries
3 tablespoons extra-virgin olive oil
2 tablespoons lime juice
½ teaspoon tamarind paste
Salt and freshly ground black
   pepper
½ cup chopped pecans, toasted
1 stalk celery, finely chopped
1 can Mandarin orange slices,
   drained (size doesn't matter, just
   add to taste)
1 15-ounce can black beans,
   rinsed and drained
2 scallions, finely chopped
1 garlic clove, crushed
½ cup finely chopped fresh
   cilantro

This grain-based salad gives you a sunny taste of the islands in the middle of winter.

1. Boil the wheat berries in a large pot with enough water to liberally cover them for about 1 hour or until they are chewy-tender. Drain.
2. In a small bowl, whisk together the oil, lime juice, and tamarind paste. Season with salt and pepper to taste.
3. Pour the wheat berries into a large bowl. Pour the dressing over and toss gently. Add remaining ingredients. Let it sit for at least 2 hours before serving, preferably at room temperature. (Please refrigerate if you are allowing it to marinate for longer than 2 hours.)

Yield: 6–8 servings

BANANA-SPELT BREAD

1 cup sugar
½ cup (1 stick) Earth Balance, at
   room temperature
1 teaspoon vanilla
1 tablespoon soy, rice, or hemp
   milk
3 very ripe bananas, mashed
1 teaspoon ground cinnamon
2 cups spelt flour
2 tablespoons soy flour
2 teaspoons baking powder
1 teaspoon baking soda
1 teaspoon salt

Optional Additions
½ cup dark chocolate chips
½ cup toasted or untoasted nuts
½ cup dried cranberries

You don't normally think of banana bread as a dessert. But serve a slice of this moist quick bread topped with a scoop of vanilla soy ice cream and a drizzle of Gianduja (see page 93) or hot fudge sauce and you may well shift the breakfast bias.

1. Preheat oven to 325°F. Grease a 9 x 5 x 3-inch loaf pan.
2. In a large mixing bowl, cream together the sugar and Earth Balance until light and fluffy. Add the vanilla and milk and mix well.
3. Mix in the mashed bananas, then add the cinnamon, flours, baking powder, baking soda and salt, a bit at a time. Mix until just combined; do not overmix. If using optional additions, stir them in by hand now.
4. Pour batter into pan and bake 60 to 70 minutes, or until a cake tester comes out clean. Cool on a rack for at least 15 minutes before inverting and removing from pan.

Yield: 10 servings

SWEET WHOLE WHEAT COUSCOUS

Most of us think of couscous for dinner, but its soft grains are the perfect texture for a quickie dessert. This recipe lends itself well to improvisation and to whatever dried fruits happen to be lurking in your pantry.

1. Add all ingredients except couscous and maple syrup/agave nectar to a large saucepan and bring to a boil. Stir in the couscous and turn off the heat. Cover and let sit for 5 or so minutes, or until couscous drinks in all the liquid. Fluff with a fork.
2. Drizzle with maple syrup or agave nectar. Serve warm.

Yield: 4 servings

2 cups coconut, almond, or hemp milk
1 teaspoon orange-flower or rose water
½ teaspoon almond extract
½ cup any of the following, or a combination: dried cranberries, raisins, currants, sultanas, dates, prunes, apples, cherries
Zest of 1 lemon or orange
Pinch salt
½ cup of your favorite chopped and (preferably) toasted nut
2 cups whole wheat couscous
Maple syrup or agave nectar for drizzling

EASY AIOLI

Aioli is a simple Provençal sauce made from mayo and garlic. It's extremely versatile and "pimps" just about any veggie, from potatoes to asparagus. You can even use it as a marinade for tofu or tempeh. I love it atop grains, especially the Golden Millet Pilaf (see page 125). It's also a fabulous sandwich spread.

1. Whisk everything in a large bowl until smooth.
2. Transfer to a glass jar. This will keep in the refrigerator for about a month—but I doubt it will last that long.

Yield: About ¾ cup

½ cup Vegenaise (please do not use other vegan mayos; this brand is crucial to the flavor)
4 garlic cloves, crushed
1 tablespoon plus 1 teaspoon white vinegar
2 teaspoons lemon juice
1 tablespoon plus 1 teaspoon extra-virgin olive oil
Salt and pepper to taste

VIN CHAUD
(HOT MULLED WINE)

1 vanilla pod, sliced in half
1 liter dry red wine
⅔ cup sugar
¼ cup water
1 orange, preferably organic, studded with cloves
2 cinnamon sticks
1 cup orange juice
¼ cup lemon juice
1 whole star anise
Pinch of nutmeg

Spend any time in Paris during the chilly winter months, and you'll see *vin chaud* stands popping up on just about every corner. My friend, Tina Chevalier, a fabulous vegan baker and gourmand, especially loves vin chaud. So I created this recipe with her in mind. Salut, Tina!

1. Using a sharp knife, scrape out the insides of the vanilla pod. Add to a large stockpot, along with everything else.
2. Bring to a boil. Reduce heat to low, and then cook uncovered for 15 to 20 minutes. Serve warm.

Yield: 6 servings

PEPPERMINT BARK

6 candy canes
1 12-ounce bag vegan white or dark chocolate chips
¼ teaspoon peppermint extract

Colorful red-and-white candy-cane shards encased in either white or dark chocolate—what could be more festive? I love savoring a piece with my after-dinner coffee. This is super simple to put together and also makes a wonderful last-minute gift.

1. Put candy canes in a plastic bag. Gently crush canes with a rolling pin. Pieces should be ¼- to ½-inch long, give or take. Just take care not to crush them into a powder!
2. Line a cookie sheet with waxed or parchment paper.
3. In a large glass bowl, melt the chips in the microwave at 50 percent power. Start at 2 minutes, then stir, and continue to nuke and then stir at 30-second intervals until the chips are melted and smooth. Stir in the peppermint extract.
4. With a spatula, pour the mixture onto the cookie sheet, then sprinkle on the candy cane pieces. Use the spatula to flatten it out to about a ¼-inch thickness. Don't worry too much about the shape.
5. Let cool and then break into "bark." To speed up the cooling process, place the cookie sheet in the freezer or fridge, depending on how harried you are.

Yield: ¾ pound of candy

MENU: COOKIES FOR SANTA

On Christmas Eve, you simply have to leave Santa a stash of cookies and a nice tall glass of soy milk. Don't forget to leave a carrot and celery out for the reindeer, too, like we did when I was a kid.

OATMEAL RAISIN COOKIES

If you find Santa's ample belly a tad bit worrying, leave the big guy some sorta', kinda' healthy Oatmeal Raisin cookies.

1. Preheat oven to 375°F. Line two cookie sheets with Silpat mats or parchment paper, or spray them with nonstick cooking spray.
2. Using a mixer, combine Earth Balance, sugars, soy milk, salt, spices, baking powder, baking soda, and vanilla. Mix until well combined, scraping down sides of bowl now and then.
3. Add flours, about ¼ cup at a time. Stir in oats, then raisins, and, if using, nuts. Dough will be stiff.
4. Drop teaspoonfuls of dough onto cookie sheets. Bake for 8 to 11 minutes or until tops start to turn golden. Cool on trays for about 1 minute then transfer to wire racks to cool completely.

Yield: About 4 dozen cookies

10 tablespoons Earth Balance, softened
⅔ cup packed brown sugar
¾ cup sugar
½ cup soy milk
½ teaspoon salt
¾ teaspoon cinnamon
¼ teaspoon ground ginger
1½ teaspoons baking powder
¼ teaspoon baking soda
1 teaspoon vanilla
1½ cups flour
⅛ cup soy flour
2 cups rolled oats
⅔ cup raisins
½ cup chopped walnuts or pecans (optional)

CLASSIC CHOCOLATE CHIPPERS

½ cup (1 stick) Earth Balance, melted

1 cup packed brown sugar

1 teaspoon vanilla

2 tablespoons soy, rice, almond, or coconut milk

⅛ teaspoon salt

½ teaspoon baking powder

¼ teaspoon baking soda

1¼ cups flour

1 heaping tablespoon soy flour

1 cup dark chocolate chips

Optional Additions

½ cup nuts

½ cup chopped dried cherries

What would Christmas be without chocolate chip cookies? Enough said. These cookies are crisp on the outside and chewy inside. Perfect dunking material.

1. Preheat oven to 375°F. Line two cookie sheets with Silpat mats or parchment paper, or spray them with nonstick cooking spray.
2. In a large mixing bowl, beat together Earth Balance, sugar, salt, vanilla, and milk until well blended.
3. Add remaining dry ingredients, about ¼ cup at a time, blending well after each addition and occasionally scraping down the side of the bowl.
4. Stir in chocolate chips and optional additions, if using.
5. Drop by tablespoonfuls onto cookie sheets. Flatten slightly with a spoon.
6. Bake 8 to 10 minutes or until golden brown. (If you used coconut milk, the baking time may be 1–2 minutes longer.)
7. Cool for 1 minute on cookie sheet, then use your spatula to transfer cookies to a wire rack. Cool for 30 minutes.

Yield: About 2 dozen cookies, recipe is easily doubled

Variations

Make these using vegan white chocolate, cinnamon, espresso, or peanut butter chips instead of chocolate.

PINE NUT COOKIES

While I'm sure that Santa loves all the classic Christmas cookies, I can't help but think he's a bit of a foodie (the potbelly is a telltale sign). These Italian half moons are sweet and nutty—just like Santa.

1. Preheat oven to 350°F. Line baking sheet with Silpat or parchment paper.
2. In a food processor, grind almonds into a very fine meal. Add sugars, flour, and salt and blend, then add extract and then Earth Balance, 1 tablespoon at a time, until a very sticky dough forms.
3. Spread pine nuts on a Silpat or waxed paper. Form dough into 1-inch balls, then roll balls in pine nuts and form into half moons.
4. Place cookies on prepared sheet and let them sit at room temperature for 1 to 2 hours before baking.
5. Bake for 15 minutes or until golden brown. Cool on rack.

Yield: 16–18 cookies

¾ cup slivered blanched almonds
1 cup sugar
2 tablespoons confectioners' sugar
2 tablespoons flour
⅛ teaspoon salt
½ teaspoon almond extract
4–6 tablespoons Earth Balance, softened
1¼ cup whole pine nuts

CHRISTMAS DAY

On Christmas morning, you want to enjoy watching the kids squeal with delight as they tear open their presents and empty their stockings. This means making Christmas breakfast ahead of time so you can be fully present. (Yes, that pun was intended, in case you wondered.)

MENU: MAKE-AHEAD CHRISTMAS BREAKFAST

PUMPKIN-MAPLE MUFFINS

These moist, seasonal muffins are tasty, yet they're packed with vitamin A, so you can feel good about eating them and sharing them with your family and friends. They freeze well, too.

Dry Ingredients

2½ cups flour
½ cup plus 2 tablespoons sugar
1 tablespoon baking powder
⅛ teaspoon salt
½ teaspoon baking soda
½ teaspoon cinnamon
½ teaspoon ground ginger
⅛ teaspoon nutmeg
1 heaping tablespoon soy flour

Wet Ingredients

¾ cup soy milk
¼ cup canola oil
1 tablespoon maple extract
1 15-ounce can unsweetened
  pumpkin puree

Optional Additions

½ cup of any of the following:
Toasted chopped walnuts, pecans,
  or almonds
Raisins
Dried or fresh cranberries
Chocolate chips

1. Preheat oven to 375°F. Line muffin tins with papers or spray lightly with cooking spray. Mix dry ingredients in a large bowl.
2. Mix wet ingredients in a medium bowl, then pour them into the dry ingredients and stir until everything is just mixed. Do not overmix or you will end up with tough muffins.
3. Stir in optional ingredients, if using. Pour into lined muffin tins.
4. Bake for 20 to 25 minutes. Cool on a rack for 5 minutes before eating.

Yield: About 16 muffins (Most people fill their muffin tins to ⅔ full, but I like to fill mine up, so you get the "overhang." It's up to you.)

SPIKED CHOCOLATE-BANANA SMOOTHIE

This is technically not a make-ahead recipe, but it's so quick and is such a necessary part of this menu. I include this smoothie—spiked with a splash of alcohol—for the parents. After enduring all of the rigors of making Christmas perfect for your loved ones, you deserve a little spot of cheer. This is a variation of my original Spiked Banana Smoothie that I included in my first cookbook. I decided to bump up the hedonism quotient by adding chocolate.

The kids can have a taste, too . . . just set some aside for them before you add the alcohol!

Process everything in the blender until smooth. If you like a thicker smoothie, add another banana or a few ice cubes. Prefer a thinner smoothie? Add more milk—or rum!

Yield: 2 large or 4 small smoothies

2 frozen very ripe bananas

2 cups chocolate soy milk

1 teaspoon vanilla, almond, or rum extract

4 tablespoons rum, coconut rum, Kahlua, crème de bananes, Tia Maria, or any other liquor that will pair with chocolate and banana (or add desired liqueur to taste)

FREEZE FRAME

As bananas turn too black to use, unpeel them and freeze them in ziplock bags. This way, you'll always have bananas on hand for smoothies or muffins.

3 tablespoons canola or safflower
oil
1 pound baking potatoes, peeled,
grated, and drained well—about
4 medium potatoes (squeeze as
much liquid as possible from the
potatoes before frying)
Salt and pepper to taste

DOWN-HOME HASH BROWNS

Crispy, carby comfort. This is a classic American breakfast dish, but I especially enjoy hash browns late at night, after a pub crawl or a long workday. Squeezing as much water as possible from the grated taters is the secret to making the hash browns crispy on the outside and tender on the inside. I love them with a dash of hot sauce.

1. Heat oil over medium heat in a large frying pan. Spread the potatoes in an even layer and season with salt and pepper.
2. Cook for about 10 to 15 minutes. Lift some of the potatoes. When they are golden, gently flip, then cook on the other side until golden.

Yield: 4 servings

EID AL-FITR

Eid al-Fitr is an Islamic feast that symbolizes the end of the month-long period of fasting called Ramadan, much in the way that Easter marks the end of Lent. People decorate their homes, visit with families, and put on the finest clothes. Most families make a donation to charities at this time.

After a month of fasting and meditation, you can work up a voracious appetite. So this menu centers on celebration, decadence, and abundance.

MENU: BREAKING THE FAST FEAST

CHICKPEAS WITH TOMATOES, EGGPLANT, AND KALE

This chickpea- and veggie-laden dish is reminiscent of something you'd find in North Africa (especially if you add harissa). It tastes best if you let it simmer on low for a few hours and allow the flavors to jam and get to know each other. This entree is substantial enough on its own, but you can also serve it over a whole grain, like brown rice, or pasta.

1. Preheat oven to 450°F. Line a cookie sheet with aluminum foil and spray it with cooking spray. Prick the eggplant all over with a fork, place on cookie sheet in heated oven and roast for about 45 minutes or until it's pooped. Remove from oven, slice in half and allow it to cool. Then scrape out the insides, chop, if needed, and set aside.
2. Combine the onion and garlic in a food processor and whir it into a paste. (Try to use a sweet onion if you can get one. It really makes a difference.)
3. In a large casserole or high-sided pan, heat oil over medium-low heat. Add onion/garlic mixture, and harissa, if using. Cook about 10 minutes, or until everything is translucent. Be careful not to burn.
4. Add remaining ingredients, including eggplant pulp but excluding the chickpeas. Bring to a boil, then lower heat to low. Cook for 1 to 2 hours, adding more oil (or water or veggie stock if you are less inclined toward decadence) as needed. This is the most important part of this dish; the longer it simmers, the better it will taste, since the flavors need to meld.
5. Add the chickpeas about 30 minutes before you want to eat. Cover and simmer, adjust the seasonings as needed, then enjoy.

Yield: 4 servings

⅓ cup olive oil

1 medium eggplant

1 large sweet onion, peeled and chopped

6 or 7 garlic cloves, peeled

Dollop of harissa (optional, but wonderful)

3 ripe large tomatoes, chopped

About 1 cup trimmed and finely chopped kale

1 teaspoon fennel seeds

1 teaspoon dried basil

1 tablespoon dried parsley

½ teaspoon dried oregano

1 15-ounce can chickpeas, rinsed and drained

Salt and pepper to taste

MUHAMMARA

¼ cup extra-virgin olive oil

1 teaspoon ground cumin

3 large red bell peppers, preferably organic, chopped

1 small onion, chopped

2 garlic cloves, crushed

1 teaspoon red pepper flakes

1¼ cup walnuts, toasted

½–1 teaspoon salt

1 tablespoon pomegranate molasses (Usually sold in Middle Eastern groceries or in gourmet shops. Substitute agave nectar if you can't find it.)

This sweet-and-spicy dip hails from Aleppo, Syria. Overflowing with vitamin A and antioxidants from the red peppers, and omega-3s from the walnuts, it's a nutritional powerhouse. Muhamarra is best known as a dip for breads and veggies, but when used as a heated sauce, it also adds an interesting element to cooked vegetable and to grilled tofu or seitan.

1. Heat the oil in a large saucepan over medium heat and add the cumin. Slowly sauté peppers, onion, garlic, and red pepper flakes until very soft. Turn down heat, if needed. The longer this sautés (without browning the garlic), the better it will taste. You can cook it up to an hour; just be sure to check the liquid level and don't let it dry out. If it seems dry, add a few tablespoons of water or vegetable broth.

2. Let cool for about 10 minutes. Pour into food processor. Add remaining ingredients and process until very smooth. If mixture is too thick, add water in 1 tablespoon increments.

Yield: 8 servings

KIBBE

Traditional kibbe are Middle Eastern meat patties made from lamb. This ovine-friendly version uses brown lentils, which have just as much protein as lamb but lack the cholesterol, fat, and meanness. Serve them with Yogurt-Tahini Sauce (see below), hummus, or the Cumin-Harissa Dipping Sauce (see page 166). But to be honest, kids will probably prefer them swimming in ketchup.

1. In a medium saucepan, bring broth to a boil. Add the bulgur, cover, and lower to heat to a simmer. Cook for 15 minutes or until bulgur is soft. Drain well.
2. Squeeze any excess moisture from the bulgur. Place it in a large bowl and add remaining ingredients (except olive oil). Mix well with your hands and be sure to "squish" the lentils. Refrigerate for at least an hour or overnight if you have time.
3. Preheat oven to 375°F. Grease a cookie sheet or line with a Silpat.
4. Form lentil mixture into 1-inch balls or 1½-inch ovals, which are more traditional. Make sure they are pressed together very tightly. Place on cookie sheet. Brush with olive oil. Bake for 15 to 20 minutes or until golden brown.

Yield: About 16 kibbe

2 cups vegetable broth
1 cup bulgur
1 cup cooked brown lentils
1 onion, very, very, very finely minced
1½ teaspoons ground cumin
½ teaspoon cinnamon
¼ teaspoon mace or nutmeg
¼ teaspoon cayenne pepper (optional)
Salt and pepper to taste
Olive oil

YOGURT-TAHINI SAUCE

This smoky, creamy sauce plays nicely against the sweet-spicy Kibbe (see above), but it also perks up cooked veggies like broccoli, spinach, and eggplant. If you thin it out a bit with some soy milk or broth, it also makes an excellent salad dressing.

Mix everything in a food processor until smooth.

Yield: 1 cup

½ cup tahini
½ cup plain soy yogurt
2 garlic cloves, crushed
4 tablespoons lemon juice
1 teaspoon sumac
¼ cup chopped fresh mint
2 tablespoons chopped fresh parsley
Salt and pepper to taste

LEMON-OLIVE TEMPEH TAGINE

10 garlic cloves, finely chopped
½ cup chopped fresh cilantro
¾ cup chopped fresh parsley
3 onions, finely chopped
3 carrots, diced
6 tablespoons olive oil
2 tablespoons sweet paprika
   (not hot)
1 tablespoon ground cumin
1 teaspoon salt
¼ teaspoon black pepper
¼ teaspoon cayenne pepper
Pinch of saffron (optional)
3 8-ounce packets tempeh,
   crumbled
1 cup oil-cured black olives, pitted
   and chopped
2 cups vegetable broth
Pepper and additional salt to taste

This dish is inspired by traditional Moroccan tagine. It's warming, filling, and perfect for sharing at a communal table. The earthiness comes courtesy of the cumin and black olives, while the lemon emits a sour undertone. Use a preserved lemon if you can find it; it really adds a distinctive flavor. (You can find them in most Middle Eastern markets. I found mine at Wegman's, a large regular grocery store.) Serve atop couscous.

1. Mix everything together in a large enamel or ovenproof pot. Toss well and let marinate for 4 hours or preferably overnight.
2. Preheat the oven to 375°F.
3. Bake covered for about 1 hour, or until everything is soft. Adjust seasonings.

Yield: 6 servings

Wine Pairing

Negro Amaro, one of the red grapes of Puglia, has a sweet-spicy finish that takes wonderfully to Moroccan flavors.

BOUGHASHA
(CIGAR-SHAPED PASTRIES)

Middle Eastern desserts are famously sweet and fragrant. They're also gorgeous stacked in pyramids on a large dessert tray. These cigar-shaped pastries are really easy to make, but anything using phyllo will make your guests think you slaved for hours. Don't even bother trying to convince them otherwise. Serve them with sweet, strong Arabic tea.

1. To make the syrup, bring the sugar, water, and lemon juice and zest to a boil. Boil until sugar dissolves completely. Add the rose or orange-flower water and allow to cool to room temperature.
2. In a small bowl, mix together the nuts, sugar, and cinnamon.
3. Preheat the oven to 375°F. Line two or three cookie sheets with Silpats.
4. To roll the "cigars," brush 1 sheet of phyllo generously (but gently) with Earth Balance. Fold it in half widthwise and brush again with Earth Balance. Fold the sheet in half once again in the same direction and brush with more Earth Balance. Evenly spread a healthy teaspoonful of the nut mixture onto this square, then gently roll it up lengthwise into a tight cigar, pinching the ends, and sealing them with a coating of Earth Balance. (**Hint:** It's easier to assemble the cigars directly on the Silpats so you don't have to move them.)
5. Once more, brush the cigar tops with any remaining Earth Balance. Bake for about 15 to 20 minutes, until slightly crisp and golden. Allow them to cool and then cut them into cigars anywhere from 1½ to 2½ inches long, depending on your preference. Place them in a deep dish and pour just enough syrup over them to dampen. Store the rest of the syrup in a small pitcher to keep those with sweet tooths in your crew (and the dentists) happy.

Yield: About 60 cigars

Syrup

2 cups sugar
1 cup water
Juice of ½ a fresh lemon
Zest of 1 organic lemon
2 teaspoons rose or orange-flower water

Pastries

3 ounces nuts, finely chopped (walnuts, pistachios, almonds, or a mixture)
3 tablespoons sugar
½ teaspoon cinnamon
8 tablespoons (1 stick) Earth Balance, melted
15 sheets vegan phyllo, thawed (See Working with Phyllo on page 9.)

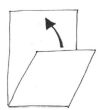
FOLD IN HALF.

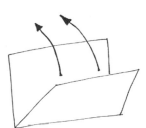
FOLD IN HALF AGAIN.

PLACE FILLING NEAR EDGE.
ROLL TOWARD UNFILLED EDGE.

TA-DA!

MILESTONE CELEBRATIONS

Life is polka-dotted with rites of passage—birthdays, weddings, and anniversaries, to name just a few. We don't wake up on the morning of these special days magically changed, but still, these rituals transform us in both apparent and subtle ways. At the very least, they cause us to stop and reflect. Appreciate what we have. Think about where we are heading and how we will get there. Some ritualistic noshing always helps fuel the reflective fire.

CHILD'S BIRTHDAY

Unlike us adults, who would prefer to forget our birthdays, kids live for them. You want to make their special day memorable, but you also want to ensure that the little partiers consume something besides cake, cookies, and candy. The goal of this menu is to feed the wee revelers a meal that you would consider at least mildly healthy. (They don't have to know this!)

MENU: KID-CENTRIC LUNCH

CHOCOLATE–PEANUT BUTTER DIP

Maybe it's the kid in me, but I'm addicted to the store-bought chocolate peanut butter. The good news is that it's easy to make, and it's a good way to ensure that kids of all ages get a shot of protein with their sugar.

Mix peanut butter, cocoa, and sweetener of your choice in the food processor until smooth. The thickness will vary, depending on the brand and kind of peanut butter you use. Just add nectar or syrup until you get the consistency you want.

Yield: 2 cups, or enough for one birthday party!

2 cups creamy natural peanut butter (no sugar added)
½ cup Dutch-process cocoa
⅓–½ cup agave nectar or maple syrup
Healthy items for dipping: whole wheat or other whole grain pretzels, banana chips, mango chips, vegan graham crackers

Variations

Substitute almond, cashew, or soy butter or raw tahini for peanut butter.

ORANGE-SOY SEITAN TENDERS

½ cup orange juice

½ cup soy sauce

⅔ cup brown sugar

Zest of 1 orange, finely chopped

1 teaspoon cumin

2 teaspoons cinnamon

About 4 cups seitan, cut into
 tenders or chunks

Kids will absolutely love the gooey orange-flavored coating on these bite-size tenders. And parents will love how easy they are to prepare.

1. Mix orange juice, soy sauce, sugar, zest, and spices in a shallow baking dish (9 x 13-inch will work). Add the seitan and toss to coat in the marinade. Cover and refrigerate for at least 3 hours or preferably overnight.
2. Preheat oven to 375°F.
3. Stir marinade and seitan well and make sure seitan sits in a single layer. Bake for 30 minutes, turn seitan pieces over, and bake for another 30 minutes.

Yield: 8–10 servings

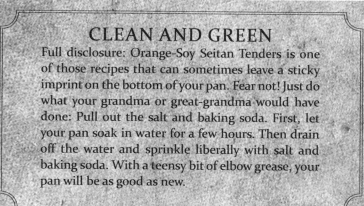

CLEAN AND GREEN

Full disclosure: Orange-Soy Seitan Tenders is one of those recipes that can sometimes leave a sticky imprint on the bottom of your pan. Fear not! Just do what your grandma or great-grandma would have done: Pull out the salt and baking soda. First, let your pan soak in water for a few hours. Then drain off the water and sprinkle liberally with salt and baking soda. With a teensy bit of elbow grease, your pan will be as good as new.

BAKED POLENTA FRIES

These grain-based fries are a fun, healthy alternative to regular french fries, and you can easily whip them up using pantry staples. If you are of the super-mom or superdad persuasion, instead of cutting these into "fries," use cookie cutters to form them into kid-wowing shapes like animals, hearts, stars, and more. Serve with ketchup or Vegenaise, or with the Cumin-Harissa Dipping Sauce (see page 166) if you're serving this to adults or adventurous kids.

6 cups broth
½ teaspoon salt
2 teaspoons dried oregano
2 teaspoons dried rosemary
1 tablespoon dried parsley
1 teaspoon garlic powder
½ cup nutritional yeast
1 cup polenta or fine cornmeal
2 tablespoons olive oil

1. Spray a large (9 x 13-inch-ish) cookie sheet with cooking spray. Use a high-sided sheet if you have one.
2. Bring the broth to a boil in a large saucepan. Add the salt, herbs, and nutritional yeast. Reduce heat to low, then whisk in the polenta, a bit at a time, taking great care to whisk away any lumps. Be very careful at this stage, because the polenta can bubble up like lava.
3. Whisk continuously until extremely thick, about 5 to 10 minutes.
4. Remove from heat. Using a spatula, spread into the prepared cookie sheet, making sure the dough is at least ½-inch thick. Let cool (place in the fridge to speed up cooling time, if you're in a hurry), then cut into fries or desired shapes. If cutting into fries, make sure they are between ½- and 1-inch wide so they will hold together. Preheat oven to 425°F.
5. Using a pastry brush, coat the tops with 1 tablespoon olive oil. Bake for 20 minutes. Turn over fries, and coat the other side with remaining oil. Bake 20 more minutes or until crispy.

Yield: A lot—enough for 4 hungry kids!

PIMP YOUR KETCHUP

Ketchup is the classic American condiment. Try these five additions (per ¼ cup of ketchup) to take your ketchup to the next level.

- ½ teaspoon tamarind paste for sweet and sour
- 1 teaspoon agave nectar plus ½ teaspoon smoked Spanish paprika for sweet and smoky
- Zest of 1 lemon or orange adds a surprising freshness
- 1 tablespoon barbecue sauce—when two American classics meet, the chemistry is unsurpassed: hot, spicy, smoky, sweet
- ½ teaspoon dark sesame oil and 1 scallion, thinly sliced—Asian meets American: smoky, dark, sweet

MUSHY PEAS

2 small onions, chopped

2 teaspoons olive oil

4 cups frozen green peas

½ cup vegan half-and-half or soy milk

2 tablespoons Earth Balance, softened

½–1 teaspoon salt

Freshly ground pepper to taste

This is classic British children's fare. With a name like "Mushy Peas," how could it not have instant kid appeal? Adults will love it, too.

1. In a small saucepan, heat the oil over medium heat and sauté the onion until soft, about 5 minutes. Set aside.

2. Fill a medium saucepan with water and bring it to a boil. Add peas and cook for 3 minutes, or until tender.

3. Drain and transfer peas to a blender or food processor. Add sautéed onion, half-and-half, Earth Balance, and salt and pepper and blend until smoothish—but don't overdo it. (Traditionally, a few peas are left whole, which further adds to the kid appeal.) If mixture is too thick, simply add a bit more half-and-half. Adjust seasonings.

Yield: 8 servings

Variations

To make a grown-up version of Mushy Peas, add any of the following while blending: about ½ cup chopped fresh mint or cilantro, 3 or 4 cloves of garlic, a dash of truffle oil, ½–1 cup chopped sautéed mushrooms.

SHIRLEY TEMPLE

Cocktails are a must for birthdays, even if you're under twenty-one. Kids will love this alcohol-free libation. And it looks so pretty in a punch bowl. My Aunt Regina used to make me a Shirley Temple on Christmas Eve so I wouldn't feel left out when all the adults were knocking back whiskey sours.

1 10-ounce jar maraschino cherries with stems
1 2-liter bottle lemon-lime soda, chilled
Ice
Orange, lemon, or lime slices

1. In a large punch bowl, mix the jar of cherries (with juice) and the soda. Add some ice.
2. To assemble a drink, pour about 1 cup into a glass, making sure it includes at least 1 cherry. Garnish with a citrus slice.

Yield: 8 servings

Variation

Add a splash of fruit-flavored syrup, like grenadine, raspberry, or pomegranate.

GROWN-UP'S BIRTHDAY

Unlike kids, most adults want nothing more than to forget their birthdays. For this reason, birthday meals for grown-ups need to be quietly dignified. Leave the old-age jokes to the greeting card writers.

MENU: MILDLY DIGNIFIED BIRTHDAY DINNER

KIWITINI

2–3 peeled, chunked kiwis
6 tablespoons agave nectar
2 tablespoons vodka
5 tablespoons dry vermouth
1 or 2 ice cubes
Fresh raspberries for garnish

It's sweet and sour. It's celadon. And it's as fun to pronounce as it is to imbibe. The kiwitini tastes just as good sans alcohol, so you can even make the kids a virgin version. But since it's your birthday, you may not feel like sharing.

Whiz everything (except raspberries) in a blender. Serve in martini glasses garnished with fresh raspberries.

Yield: 2 servings

LETTUCE SOUP

2 tablespoons olive oil
1 cup chopped onions
3 garlic cloves, chopped
1 teaspoon cumin
¼ teaspoon ground coriander
½ teaspoon salt
¼ teaspoon white pepper
1 large potato, peeled and diced
8 cups chopped lettuce
3 cups broth

Lettuce is one food Americans are used to eating only raw. But the fact is that most lettuces, including the ill-reputed iceberg, have a very creamy, rich nature that heat somehow teases out. Of course, the fresher the lettuce you use, the better the taste. But if you're watching your pennies (and who isn't, these days?), this is a good use for lettuce that looks just a tad weary, and the taste difference is nominal.

1. Heat oil in a large soup pan over medium heat. Sauté the onion and garlic until soft, about 5 minutes. Sprinkle in the cumin, coriander, and salt, and sauté another minute or so.
2. Add remaining ingredients and bring to a boil. Reduce heat, cover, and simmer until the potato is very soft, about 15 minutes.
3. Puree carefully in batches in a blender or use an immersion blender. Adjust seasonings.

Yield: 3 servings

ROASTED SPAGHETTI SQUASH

Is it a side dish or an entree? This is the carbo-phobic pasta lover's best friend. It's fabulous tossed with some good and garlicky marinara, a classic marinara, or even a vegan carbonara. But I think it's made for the Sweet-and-Sour Balsamic Glaze (see below). Top with toasted pine nuts—a must!

1 medium spaghetti squash
1 tablespoon olive oil
Salt and pepper to taste
1 recipe Sweet-and-Sour Balsamic Glaze (see below)
About ⅓ cup whole, toasted pine nuts

1. Preheat oven to 350°F. Cut a large (5-inch) slit in the squash and place it on a foil-lined tray in the preheated oven, slit-side up, for about 15 to 30 minutes (depending on the size of the squash) to soften the skin.
2. Remove from oven and when cool enough, using a large knife or machete (kidding! Stick with the large knife please), cut the squash in half lengthwise. Be very careful because it's a tough little squash.
3. Remove seeds and stringy fibers with a fork. Drizzle with olive oil and season with salt and pepper.
4. Roast cut side down for about 45 minutes. Remove from oven, flip, and then roast cut side up for an additional 10 to 15 minutes, or until squash easily becomes "spaghetti" when gently flaked with a fork.
5. Top each serving of spaghetti squash with the glaze and toasted pine nuts.

Yield: 4–6 servings

Wine Pairing

Garganega-based wines from the Veneto—Soave and Custoza—are medium-bodied, a little nutty, and are brilliant with most squash dishes.

SWEET-AND-SOUR BALSAMIC GLAZE

I'm not going to lie to you: This is an intense sauce, not for the faint of heart. It's sweet. It's sour. And it looks like chocolate. It's very rich, so a little goes a long way. Although it's made especially to pair with the Roasted Spaghetti Squash (see above), it also makes an unusual-but-tasty barbecue sauce for marinated pressed tofu or steamed tempeh. I also like a bit drizzled on sweet potatoes or sweet potato fries.

3 tablespoons olive oil
7 garlic cloves, minced
4 tablespoons (about ½ of a 6-ounce can) tomato paste
½ cup good-quality balsamic vinegar
½ cup raisins
½ cup agave nectar
1 cup water, divided
2 tablespoons Earth Balance
Salt and pepper to taste

1. Heat the oil in a saucepan over medium heat. Sauté garlic until soft, about 5 minutes.
2. Add tomato paste and stir, letting it color the oil, about 3 minutes.
3. Stir in the balsamic vinegar and the raisins, stirring constantly. The sauce should thicken quickly and will look like melted chocolate.
4. At this point, add ½ cup of the water and agave nectar. Again, continue stirring. When this has reduced by half, repeat this step, once again, adding ½ cup water and 2 tablespoons Earth Balance, stirring until reduced.
5. Pour over spaghetti squash to serve.

Yield: About ½ cup sauce, enough for 1 recipe of Roasted Spaghetti Squash

BROWNIE-GIANDUJA CAKE WITH CHOCOLATE-GRAVITAS FROSTING

Brownie-Gianduja Cake

14 tablespoons (1 stick plus 6 tablespoons) Earth Balance, softened

3 cups sugar

1½ tablespoons vinegar

2 teaspoons vanilla

1¼ cups cocoa

2 tablespoons espresso powder

2 teaspoons baking powder

2 teaspoons baking soda

1 teaspoon salt

3 cups flour

¼ cup soy flour

3 cups soy milk

1 recipe Gianduja (see page 93) or 1 12.3-ounce jar vegan chocolate-hazelnut spread

1 recipe Chocolate-Gravitas Frosting (see page 149)

This is a once-a-year indulgence: two layers of dense, brownie-like chocolate cake, sandwiched with a vegan Nutella-type spread, and liberally iced with a coffee-chocolate buttercream. Warning: This cake is extremely rich.

1. Preheat oven to 350°F. Grease three 8-inch cake pans and dust lightly with flour.
2. Cream together Earth Balance, sugar, vinegar, and vanilla.
3. In a large bowl, sift together remaining dry ingredients.
4. Alternate beating in dry ingredients and soy milk, in about ½- to 1-cup increments. Beat until smooth.
5. Pour into prepared cake pans, filling each about ⅔ full.
6. Bake for 40 to 50 minutes or until tester comes out clean. Let cool completely on wire racks before removing from pans.
7. To assemble the cake, place one cake layer on a flat surface. Spread Gianduja liberally on top. Place a second cake layer over this and spread with more Gianduja. Top with the third cake layer. Frost cake top and sides with Chocolate-Gravitas Frosting and decorate, if desired (see Top Stuff, page 149).

Yield: About 16 servings

CHOCOLATE-GRAVITAS FROSTING

This coffee-chocolate buttercream icing is hedonistic, finger-licking good,, and worthy of any celebration—or just because it's Tuesday!

1. Cream together Earth Balance and cocoa.
2. Alternate adding sifted confectioners' sugar and liquid, a few tablespoons at a time. Mix well until spreadable and no lumps remain.

Yield: Enough frosting for a 3-layer cake or about 18 cupcakes

10 tablespoons (½ stick plus 2 tablespoons) Earth Balance, softened
¾ cup cocoa
4 cups confectioners' sugar, sifted
Up to ½ cup espresso (you can just use coffee or soy milk, but you'll miss out on the "gravitas" that comes with espresso)
Pinch of salt

TOP STUFF

To make this cake birthday-ready and extra-fancy, you need to decorate it. Of course, you can (ho-hum!) write "Happy Birthday, John Doe" with an icing pen. But this little trick makes for a much more elegant finish: Melt about ¼ cup chocolate chips or buttons. Pour them into a plastic bag or, preferably, a waxed paper bag. Carefully snip a very small hole in one end (do this right next to the cake) and drizzle the top of the cake à la Jackson Pollack with random swirls and drips. Or if you're more of the patisserie persuasion, make concentric circles, crisscrosses, or lines.

WEDDING

A marriage is a real cause for celebration. What could be happier than two people finding true love? The food should be light, tasty, and symbolic of the couple's new life together.

MENU: WEDDING FEAST

BRUSCHETTA WITH EASY ROMESCO SAUCE

Easy Romesco Sauce

1 small chile pepper
1 cup roasted red peppers, drained
1 slice stale bread, crust removed
2 tablespoons nutritional yeast
4 garlic cloves
2 tomatoes, seeded and chopped
½ cup almonds
5 tablespoons olive oil
2 tablespoons red wine vinegar
Salt and pepper to taste

Bruschetta

1 loaf French or Italian bread
Basil leaves and Marcona almonds
  for garnish

This gorgeous red Spanish sauce is extremely tasty—and extremely versatile. You can use it as a dip or spread or toss it with pasta. It also makes a great topping for grilled tofu, tempeh, or seitan. Here, it's used as an elegant bruschetta topper.

1. Process everything for the sauce until smooth in the food processor.
2. Slice bread very thinly (about ¼-inch thick) and toast on cookie sheet in a 350°F oven for about 10 minutes.
3. Spread Easy Romesco Sauce on bread. Top with a basil leaf and a Marcona almond.

Yield: About 30 appetizers

Wine Pairing
Italians would drink Prosecco, Spanish would drink Cava;
either sparkling wine will get your dinner party started right.

PENNE WITH VODKA SAUCE

This recipe has all the richness you except in a celebratory dish, plus it's very easy to make and it's easy to double or triple for larger quantities. Since it's so decadent, a small serving, along with a fresh tossed salad, is all you need to serve. Besides, all your guests really care about is the dessert. I love the pale pink color, just like a blushing bride. Except that brides don't blush anymore.

1. Melt Earth Balance along with oil in a large sauté pan over medium heat. Add chopped onion and garlic. Sauté until soft, about 5 minutes.
2. Add tomatoes and simmer over medium heat until almost all the liquid is cooked off, about 25 minutes, stirring frequently.
3. Whisk in vegan cream, vodka, and red pepper flakes. Bring to a boil and cook for about 2 minutes or until sauce thickens. Season to taste with salt and pepper. Add pasta and toss to cover. Add basil and nutritional yeast.

Yield: 4–6 servings

1 tablespoon Earth Balance
1 tablespoon olive oil
1 onion, very finely chopped
6 garlic cloves, crushed
1 28-ounce can plum tomatoes, drained, seeded, and chopped
1 cup vegan cream
¼ cup vodka
¼ teaspoon crushed red pepper flakes
Salt and pepper to taste
1 pound penne pasta, cooked according to package directions
½ cup finely chopped fresh basil
¼ cup nutritional yeast, plus more for sprinkling

Wine Pairing
Try a crisp Italian white, such as Trebbiano d'Abbruzo.

MEXICAN WEDDING COOKIES

1 cup (2 sticks) Earth Balance, at
  room temperature
½ cup plus 1½ cups
  confectioners' sugar
½ teaspoon salt
2 teaspoons vanilla
2 cups flour
1 cup pecans, almonds, or walnuts
  (or a combination), toasted and
  finely ground into a flour
¼ teaspoon cinnamon

White and innocent, these tasty cinnamon-infused cookies look lovely arranged in a pyramid, with randomly inserted roses, as part of a wedding dessert display. They're also very easy to make.

1. Beat Earth Balance, ½ cup confectioners' sugar, salt, and vanilla together in large bowl until fluffy. Beat in flour, about ½ cup at a time, and then add the nut flour. Divide the dough in half; form each half into ball. Wrap separately in waxed paper and refrigerate for about 1 hour.
2. Preheat oven to 350°F. Line a large baking sheet (or two) with a Silpat or spray with cooking spray.
3. Place remaining confectioners' sugar in a large, shallow bowl or dish and mix in the cinnamon.
4. Working with half of chilled dough, roll dough into approximately 1½-inch balls. Place cookies on prepared baking sheet, spacing them ½ inch apart. Bake until just golden on top, and golden on underside, about 16 to 18 minutes.
5. Cool for 5 minutes, then gently roll in confectioners' sugar mixture. Set on wire racks to cool completely. Repeat with remaining dough.
6. Sift remaining confectioners' sugar mixture over cookies before serving.

Yield: 46–50 cookies

ANNIVERSARY

Sure, it's fun to go out to dinner on your anniversary, but staying in can be even more romantic and tasty, especially if you prepare the meal together. Set the mood with candles, soft jazz, and ambient lighting (dimmer switches are your friends).

MENU: ROMANTIC ANNIVERSARY DINNER

PAN-SEARED TOFU WITH BASIL-BALSAMIC GLAZE

With its faint licorice scent and the garlic's sweet depth, this dish screams elegance and sophistication. Don't tell anyone how easy it is to make! This tofu also makes an excellent sandwich filling.

1. Mix all ingredients except the extra 1 tablespoon olive oil, tofu, and garnish in a shallow pan. Add pressed tofu slices, and flip to ensure all sides are basted with the marinade. Marinade for at least 2 hours or overnight, turning occasionally and basting with more marinade.
2. Heat 1 tablespoon oil in a large frying pan over medium heat. (If you are using a nonstick pan, you'll only need a tiny drizzle of oil.)
3. Fry tofu until slightly charred, about 4 to 5 minutes on each side, adding more glaze/marinade if needed.
4. Garnish with fresh basil.

Yield: 4 servings

6 tablespoons plus 1 tablespoon extra-virgin olive oil
5–6 tablespoons minced fresh basil
2 tablespoons best-quality balsamic vinegar
2 tablespoons soy sauce
¼ cup fresh lemon juice
4 garlic cloves, finely minced
1 pound extra-firm tofu, pressed for 2 hours and cut into 4 triangles or squares (see page xi)
Fresh basil leaves for garnish

GREEN BEANS AND EDAMAME WITH DIJON-YOGURT

1 pound green beans, trimmed
  and cut into 1½-inch pieces
2 cups frozen shelled edamame
½ cup plain soy yogurt
½ tablespoon lemon juice
Zest of 1 lemon
1 tablespoon Dijon mustard
1 teaspoon soy sauce
1 teaspoon agave nectar or maple
  syrup
Dash of red pepper flakes
Salt and pepper to taste

The brightness and slight sweetness of crisp green beans and edamame contrast with the sourness of the Dijon-laced yogurt. Serve this at room temperature.

1. Bring a large pot of salted water to boil. Toss in green beans and edamame, and cook to desired level of crispness. (I prefer tender-crisp, about 3 to 4 minutes.) Drain well and place under cold water to stop the cooking.
2. Whisk remaining ingredients together and toss with the green beans and edamame. Adjust seasonings.

Yield: 6 servings

PEAR TARTE TATIN

With its gorgeous concentric circles of ginger-scented pears, this dessert is a seasonal alternative to the more traditional apple tarte tatin. It provides the elegant "wow" factor required for a special-occasion dessert. And it's not as difficult as you may imagine!

Serve this warm with soy ice cream and/or a drizzle of chocolate sauce. Don't be afraid of inverting the tarte. The trick is to let the tarte cool for a few minutes, clear the edges with a knife, and then quickly and confidently flip it onto a dish.

1. Preheat oven to 425°F.
2. Peel, core, and quarter the pears. Toss in a medium bowl with lemon juice.
3. On stove top, melt 2 tablespoons Earth Balance in a 9-inch cake pan or cast-iron pan. Remove from heat and sprinkle with 4 tablespoons brown sugar. Arrange pears on top of brown sugar in a tight, concentric circle, then dot with remaining Earth Balance and sprinkle with 4 tablespoons brown sugar, ginger, and cinnamon.
4. Cook on stove top over medium heat until a loose caramel starts to form (about 20 minutes).
5. Place in oven for 5 minutes to cook the tops of the pears.
6. Mix all pastry ingredients together and roll out to a 10-inch disk. Place over top of the pears and trim or tuck in the edges.
7. Bake for 18 to 20 minutes, or until the crust is golden.
8. Remove from heat and cool on a rack for 5 minutes. Trace the edge of the pan with a knife to loosen any dough that might be sticking. Place a large plate over the top of the tarte and quickly flip the pan. Before removing the cake dish, tap to loosen any remnants that might be sticking. (This should not be a problem if you use enough Earth Balance.)

Yield: 6 servings

Tarte Filling

5 Bosc or Bartlett pears
2 tablespoons lemon juice
6 tablespoons Earth Balance
8 tablespoons brown sugar, divided
½ teaspoon ground ginger
½ teaspoon cinnamon

Sweet Pastry

2 cups whole wheat pastry flour, plus a few more tablespoons for rolling out dough
8 tablespoons Earth Balance
4 tablespoons confectioners' sugar
6–8 tablespoons soy or rice milk
¼ teaspoon salt

FUNERAL

Although funerals are sad rituals, at least in our culture, they are still celebrations—of lives well lived and people well loved and admired. Food is designed to reaffirm life and to comfort the mourners during a difficult time. Sharing a meal with family and friends is a strengthening event. It demonstrates that life goes on, but also, that love transcends everything, even death.

MENU: CELEBRATION OF A LIFE

HUMBLE AND HEARTY VEGETABLE SOUP

2 tablespoons olive oil
1 large onion, chopped
5 garlic cloves, sliced
1 carrot, diced
1 stalk celery, diced
8 cups vegetable stock
1 bay leaf
2 tablespoons dried parsley
1 teaspoon dried rosemary
1 teaspoon dried oregano
¼ teaspoon red pepper flakes
Salt and pepper to taste
2 cups trimmed and roughly
   chopped kale or spinach
1 or 2 potatoes, peeled and diced
2 cups cooked chickpeas or 1
   15-ounce can chickpeas, drained
   and rinsed
1 cup uncooked barley

Optional Additions
½ cup fresh or frozen corn,
   edamame, or peas
Squeeze of fresh lemon juice

Nothing is as comforting as breaking bread with people you love and supping on this filling soup in memory and in honor of a loved one. It's reminiscent of something your grandmother would make and, like all vegetable soups, is extremely forgiving. So don't be afraid to play around with the proportions.

1. Heat oil in a large stockpot over medium-low heat. Sauté onions, garlic, carrots, and celery until soft, about 5 to 10 minutes.
2. Add remaining ingredients and bring to a rolling boil.
3. Lower heat to a simmer and cook partially covered until carrots and potatoes are soft, about 45 minutes. Add corn, edamame, or peas and/ or lemon juice before serving.

Yield: 8 hearty servings

FUNERAL CASSEROLE

Believe it or not, when researching this chapter, I ran across a cookbook that focuses on funeral foods. It's called *Being Dead Is No Excuse: The Official Southern Ladies Guide to Hosting the Perfect Funeral,* a great title to say the least, and a lovely gesture to console those in mourning with an entire cookbook filled with comforting foods. But sadly, most traditional funeral foods are chock-full of the kinds of unhealthy recipes that cause more premature funerals. This casserole recipe is no-nonsense, unpretentious comfort food. It's easy to prepare for a crowd, but it is also semi-healthy while being comforting, because the dearly departed want you to live a long and healthy life.

1. Preheat oven to 375°F.
2. Place the flour in a shallow dish and dredge the tempeh in the flour.
3. Heat the oil over medium heat in a large sauté pan and brown the tempeh, turning once or twice during the cooking process. Place browned tempeh in a 9 x 13-inch baking dish.
4. Sauté the onion, garlic, peppers, and celery in the oil until soft, about 10 minutes. Add the corn and spinach and cook for another 10 minutes.
5. In a small bowl, whisk together the ketchup, broth, brown sugar, soy sauce, and parsley.
6. Pour sauce over tempeh. Add cooked vegetables and stir. Bake for 15 to 20 minutes or until warmed through.

Yield: 6 servings, recipe is easily doubled

½ cup whole wheat pastry flour

2 8-ounce packages tempeh, cut into cubes and steamed for 10 minutes (see page xi)

2 tablespoons olive oil

1 cup chopped onion

3 garlic cloves, chopped

2 organic green peppers, chopped

3 stalks celery, chopped

3 cups corn (frozen is fine)

2 cups chopped spinach

½ cup ketchup

½ cup vegetable broth

¼ cup brown sugar

2 tablespoons soy sauce

3 tablespoons dried parsley

FUNERAL CAKE

This cake is very simple to put together and is comforting in its simplicity. Traditionally made to take to the mourner's house as a gesture of caring, it's rich, damp, and chocolaty. You can ice it or glaze it if you want, but really, this cake is perfect as it is, perhaps dusted with a bit of confectioners' sugar to prettify.

½ teaspoon vinegar
½ cup rice or soy milk
2 cups sugar
2 cups flour
2 tablespoons soy flour
1 teaspoon baking soda
½ teaspoon cinnamon
¼ teaspoon salt
1 cup water
½ cup (1 stick) Earth Balance
½ cup canola oil
5 tablespoons cocoa
1 teaspoon vanilla
Confectioners' sugar for dusting
  (optional)

1. Grease a 13 x 9 x 2-inch pan. Preheat oven to 400°F.
2. Add vinegar to milk. Set aside and allow to curdle.
3. Meanwhile, in a large bowl stir together sugar, flours, baking soda, cinnamon, and salt.
4. In a large saucepan, bring water, Earth Balance, oil, and cocoa to a boil.
5. Pour cocoa-water mixture over dry ingredients, mix well, then stir in the curdled milk and vanilla.
6. Pour into prepared pan and bake for 25 to 30 minutes or until cake tester comes out clean.
7. Cool on a rack and cut into squares. Dust with confectioners' sugar, if desired.

Yield: 16 servings

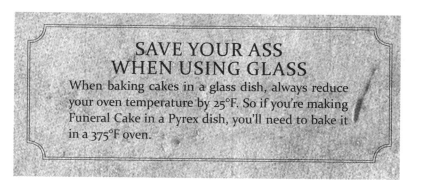

SAVE YOUR ASS
WHEN USING GLASS
When baking cakes in a glass dish, always reduce your oven temperature by 25°F. So if you're making Funeral Cake in a Pyrex dish, you'll need to bake it in a 375°F oven.

EVERYDAY CELEBRATIONS

The concept of "everyday celebrations" reads as an oxymoron, like "liquid gas" or "student teacher." But still, I love the concept and the conundrum: Every day can and should be a celebration. After all, we are alive. We are lucky. There are a million reasons to celebrate, whether it's because Mother Nature sent down two feet of snow and forced businesses and schools to close, or because we found a precious slot of time to share a cup of tea with our best friends.

GIRLS' NIGHT IN

Lisa. Claire. Violet. Pam. What would I do without my girlfriends? Not only do they make me belly laugh, but they have also helped me through some of the toughest times of my life. So invite your girlfriend posse over and fete them with this BFF menu.

MENU: GIRLY-GIRL FEAST

POMEGRANATE COSMO

1–2 tablespoons vodka
1½ teaspoons Cointreau, Grand
   Marnier, or triple sec (in order
   of my preference)
1½ teaspoons fresh lime juice
2 tablespoons pomegranate juice
Fresh pomegranate seeds and a
   lime wedge for garnish

Cosmopolitans are the perfect balance of sweet and sour ingredients—and are the ultimate accessory. Variety is the spice of life, so once in a while, I like to make my Cosmo using puckery pomegranate juice instead of the more traditional cranberry.

Shake all ingredients except garnish with ice in a cocktail mixer. Strain into a martini glass. Add seeds and lime wedge.

Yield: 1 serving

SUBSTANTIAL MIX-AND-MATCH SALAD

Page through any cooking magazine or cookbook (ahem!), and you'll run across hundreds of salad recipes. I must confess, I'm a serial salad improviser, especially during the hot summer months when I call salad "dinner" at least two or three nights each week. (Weird but true: I have also been known to nosh on salad for breakfast.) Through my experimentation, I've found that the best salads are always a mosaic of colors, flavors, and textures: sweet, salt, and starch—and sometimes bitter (think endive or radicchio), all tossed together with fresh, tender greens (well rinsed and dried, please). We Americans tend to oversoak our salads in dressing, so I challenge you to exercise restraint and just coat your salad with dressing. This way, you'll experience the intense flavors of the vegetables and other ingredients. Use the following chart to get started. The possibilities are endless!

Choose one element from each of the listed categories. Toss with your favorite salad dressing, or try one of the dressing recipes that follow on pages 162–163. When dressing your salad, do as the French do: Use just enough to coat the salad ingredients. Et voilà!

Yield: 1 large salad, enough for 4 as a side or 2 for dinner

Base

4 cups of any of the following, or a mixture:

Arugula

Boston lettuce

Endive

Frisée

Green or red leaf lettuce

Mâche (unfortunately, it's not widely available in the United States; Trader Joe's usually sells it. Grab it if you see it.)

Organic baby spinach

Radicchio

Romaine lettuce

Shredded cabbage (red, green, or Napa)

Sweet

¼–⅓ cup of any of the following:

Dried cranberries

Halved grapes

Cubed persimmon

Pomegranate seeds

Raisins

Whole raspberries

Sliced apples

Sliced banana

Sliced pears

Chopped strawberries

Diced watermelon

Crunchy

¼–⅓ cup of any of the following, or a mixture:

Croutons (toss day-old, whole grain bread or pita with some olive oil and your favorite herbs; bake at 350°F until dry and golden, about 10 minutes)

Crumbled crispbread, tortilla chips, whole grain pretzels, or crackers

Your favorite toasted or untoasted nuts (walnuts, pistachios, almonds, pecans)

Your favorite toasted or untoasted seeds (sunflower, pumpkin, squash)

Color

1 cup of any of the following, or a mixture:

Cooked corn

Cooked, cubed winter squash

Halved grape tomatoes

Peas

Radishes (these can be overpowering, so limit to ½ cup)

Shredded carrots

Sliced red or golden beets

Thinly sliced cucumbers

Thinly sliced zucchini or yellow squash

Chopped tomatoes

Protein

1 cup of any of the following, or a mixture:

Cooked mushrooms

Cooked, drained chickpeas, lentils, or beans

Cooked, shelled edamame

Pan-fried or baked tofu or tempeh (a great way to resurrect leftovers)

Optional Additions

Up to ½ cup of any of the following:

Artichoke hearts, drained

Shredded Daiya cheese

Sun-dried tomatoes, drained

Optional Toppings

Capers, rinsed well

Chopped olives

Ground flaxseed (great nutty flavor plus important omega-3s)

Nutritional yeast

SPICY TOMATO-LEMON DRESSING

3 tablespoons tomato paste

3 tablespoons extra-virgin olive oil

3 tablespoons fresh-squeezed
lemon juice

¼ cup water

1 garlic clove, crushed

1 tablespoon agave nectar

¼–½ teaspoon harissa, or to
taste

Salt and pepper to taste

Spicy, sweet, and sour—all rolled up into an easy salad dressing that you can whip up using pantry staples. It pairs nicely with creamy greens like cabbage and iceberg lettuce (which, despite its lack of nutrition, is still tasty, and therefore an occasional guilty pleasure of mine). One of my recipe testers described this as a sort of "Arabic ketchup." That said, you can also use it as a condiment.

Mix everything in a tightly sealed glass jar, and shake, shake, shake.

Yield: About ½ cup (will keep in the refrigerator for about 1 week)

⅓ cup Vegenaise

1 tablespoon Dijon mustard

1 tablespoon plus 1 teaspoon
agave nectar

1 garlic clove, crushed

½ teaspoon lemon juice

Salt and pepper to taste

AGAVE-MUSTARD DRESSING

This sweet and tangy dressing tastes especially good over plump baby spinach or mâche. It also pairs well with bitter greens like endive, frisée, and radicchio. It also works well as a dipping sauce; try it with the Cornflake-Seitan Nuggets (see page 170).

Whisk everything together in a small bowl.

Yield: About ½ cup, enough for a family dinner salad

POPPY-SEED DRESSING

It's fun to encounter the little black poppy seeds polka-dotting your salad. Just be sure to check your teeth after indulging.

Whisk everything together in a small bowl. Let sit for a few hours before serving to allow the flavors to meld. Store in a tightly closed jar.

Yield: About ½ cup

½ cup olive oil
⅓ cup maple syrup
3 tablespoon cider vinegar
1 tablespoon grated onion
1 garlic clove, crushed
1 tablespoon Dijon mustard
1 teaspoon poppy seeds
1 teaspoon lemon juice
1 garlic clove, crushed
Salt and pepper to taste

DOUBLE-GINGER WHITE-MISO DRESSING

Whole Foods sells a Philadelphia-made ginger-miso dressing that I am unabashedly addicted to. I use it as a salad dressing, dipping sauce, and marinade. This is my shameless attempt to replicate it based on the cruel fact that it costs $5.50 a bottle.

Whiz everything together in a food processor until very smooth.

Yield: 1 cup

1-inch piece ginger, peeled and chopped
2 tablespoons pickled ginger (sushi ginger), drained
6 tablespoons white miso
6 tablespoons extra-virgin olive oil
1 teaspoon soy sauce
2 teaspoons rice wine vinegar
2 tablespoons agave nectar
1 tablespoon lemon juice
1 clove garlic, peeled and chopped
1 tablespoon water (more or less, add more if you prefer a thinner dressing; omit if you prefer a thicker dressing)

6 apples, peeled, cored, and
   chopped
1 cup sugar
½ cup packed brown sugar
2 cups rolled oats
Lots of cinnamon (I would say
   about 2 teaspoons)
About 6 tablespoons (¾ stick)
   Earth Balance, softened
Pinch of salt

TRAIL VIEW INN
APPLE CRUMBLE

This apple crumble is sweet, spicy, and comforting, just like your best friends. It's the perfect dish to share, especially when warmed and topped with a large scoop of vanilla soy ice cream. I got this recipe from the nice folks who run the vegan-friendly Trail View Inn (www.trailviewinn.com) in New York's Catskill Mountains, where I once stayed while skiing. The only thing I added was a pinch of salt to counter all the yummy sugar!

1. Preheat oven to 450°F.
2. Place apples in a greased 9 x 9-inch pan. Mix remaining ingredients in a large bowl to create a crumble, and scatter evenly over apples.
3. Bake for 25 to 30 minutes until golden on top and bubbling.

Yield: 6 servings

TAILGATE PARTY

The tailgate party is an all-American tradition. What's better than enjoying good food and tasty drinks before the big game? Enjoying vegan food and drinks, of course.

MENU: TAILGATE TREATS

SPICY SEITAN WINGS

These are kinder, gentler wings that are equally as portable and much healthier than their deep-fried nonvegan counterparts. Best of all, you can whip them up in about fifteen minutes of hands-on time. The thinner you form it, the crispier the wing, so adjust the shapes to fit your preferences. Don't get all Martha Stewart about the shapes. These wings are like wrapping paper at Christmas; they'll be gone so fast that no one will notice what they look like! Serve them with the Cumin-Harissa Dipping Sauce (see page 166) or with your own favorite dipping sauce.

1 cup instant vital wheat gluten
3 tablespoons nutritional yeast
½ teaspoon salt
1 teaspoon cayenne pepper
1 teaspoon sweet paprika
½ teaspoon garlic powder
¾–1 cup vegetable broth
2 tablespoons barbecue sauce
2 tablespoons olive oil plus about 4 tablespoons for drizzling

1. Preheat oven to 350°F. Drizzle a 9 x 13-inch baking dish or cookie sheet with olive oil (about 1½ tablespoons).
2. In a large bowl, mix all ingredients together except the oil for drizzling. Start with ¾ cup of broth and add more if the dough seems dry. Knead in the bowl until fairly smooth and everything is well incorporated.
3. Form into "wings" or nuggets. You can actually mimic the shape of a wing, but this creeps me out, so I just form them into pieces that measure approximately 1 x ½ inches.
4. Place pieces in prepared dish and drizzle with remaining oil. Toss to coat (I use my fingers).
5. Bake for 15 to 20 minutes (depending on your crispness preference), turning halfway through.
6. Cool for 5 minutes before serving. If you need to reheat these, please do not microwave them. Warm them, covered, in a 250°F oven for about 10 minutes.

Yield: 28–32 pieces

Variation

In step 4, you can coat with a flavored oil or with your favorite barbecue sauce. If using barbecue sauce, you will probably need to toss the wings in at least ¾ to 1 cup.

½ cup Vegenaise
1 teaspoon cumin
1 tablespoon agave nectar
½–3 tablespoons harissa
¼ teaspoon salt

CUMIN-HARISSA DIPPING SAUCE

This easy sauce was designed specifically to accompany the Spicy Seitan Wings (see page 165), but this also makes a great marinade or sauce for grilled tofu or steamed tempeh. It's also an excellent stand-in for mayo. This sauce is very spicy, so start with ½ tablespoon of harissa and keep adding until you have reached your desired level of heat.

Whisk everything together in a small bowl.

Yield: About ½ cup

10 cups popped popcorn
1 cup of your favorite salted nuts (chopped peanuts, chopped walnuts, sliced almonds)
1 cup light or dark corn syrup
4 tablespoons (½ stick) Earth Balance
2 cups dark chocolate chips or buttons
1 teaspoon vanilla
¼ teaspoon salt

CHOCOLATE POPCORN

Don't sweat too much about exact measurements. This recipe is very forgiving. Think about it: When you mix chocolate, popcorn, and Earth Balance in any proportion, it's got to be good. I doubt there will be any leftovers when you're tailgating, but in the event there are, store them in an airtight tin for up to two weeks.

1. Preheat oven to 300°F. Grease a roasting pan. Pour the popcorn and nuts in the pan.
2. In a large saucepan, melt together corn syrup, Earth Balance, chocolate, and vanilla over medium heat. Add salt. Bring the mixture to a boil, stirring constantly for a few minutes. Be very careful not to let the hot molten candy splash you while it cooks.
3. Pour the molten chocolate over the popcorn and nuts. Use a spatula and mix well. Don't worry if everything does not end up coated; it probably won't. The idea is to get some chocolaty goodness in every bite. Bake for about 15 minutes.
4. If you want to speed up the cooling time, place in the refrigerator.

Yield: 6 servings

Variations

Add 2 teaspoons cinnamon for Mexican-Chocolate Popcorn.
Add 1 tablespoon finely grated orange zest for Orange-Chocolate Popcorn.
Add ¼ teaspoon cayenne (or to taste) for Spicy-Chocolate Popcorn.
Add ½ cup of any of the following: dried cranberries, dried cherries, broken-up pretzels.

TEA TIME

Yin to the tailgate party's yang, afternoon tea is the perfect time to catch up on gossip—or the latest theory on quantum physics. The topic of discussion is not as important as the close circle of friends you choose to surround yourself with, and of course, the tea and traditional dainty treats that you serve.

MENU: TEA PARTY

CUCUMBER SANDWICHES

If you're having a bona fide tea party, then you have to serve tea sandwiches. These dainty little 'wiches are rather austere and dignified. You'll want to hold out your pinky while you indulge. They are also quite figure friendly, presumably since you will want to save your calories for the scrumptious tea party desserts. Remember: Tea sandwiches are petite, so from a single slice of bread you can probably get three sandwiches. You can also use cookie cutters to create fancy sandwich shapes, like hearts, stars, and fleur-de-lis. Tea sandwiches taste best when made with very thin bread.

1 cucumber, peeled and thinly sliced (use a mandoline if you have one)
½ cup (1 stick) Earth Balance, softened
2 garlic cloves, crushed
Salt and pepper to taste
16 thin slices bread of choice
2 teaspoons lemon juice
1 tablespoon extra-virgin olive oil

1. Drain the cukes well by letting them sit in a colander for 30 minutes, and remove the crusts from the bread (save them in a ziplock bag for bread crumbs).
2. Mix the Earth Balance and garlic. Season with salt and pepper.
3. In a shallow bowl, mix lemon juice and olive oil. Gently toss the cucumber slices to coat.
4. To assemble the sandwiches, butter each slice of bread with the Earth Balance mixture. Cover one slice of buttered bread with cukes and top with another slice.
5. Cut each "normal-size" sandwich into thirds. Or use a cookie cutter at this point to cut into desired shapes.

Yield: About 24 wee 'wiches

CHILLED WATERCRESS-SPINACH SOUP

2 tablespoons extra-virgin olive oil

I cup very thinly sliced leeks (save a few slivers for garnish)

I shallot, chopped

I potato, peeled and diced

2 cups vegetable broth

I cup plain soy yogurt (reserve about I tablespoon for garnish)

2 cups packed chopped watercress (save a few pieces for garnish)

1½ cups chopped baby spinach

I teaspoon lemon juice

½ teaspoon lemon zest

Salt and freshly ground pepper to taste

Watercress is the quintessential tea party veggie. Serving this creamy soup chilled, along with room-temperature finger sandwiches, is a nice counterpoint to all the hot tea you'll be sipping.

1. Heat the oil over medium heat in a large stockpot. Sauté the leeks and shallot until soft, about 5 minutes.
2. Add the remaining ingredients and bring to a boil. Reduce heat, cover, and simmer for about 15 minutes, or until potatoes are very soft.
3. Carefully puree using either a blender or an immersion blender. Chill for several hours or preferably overnight.
4. Just before serving, garnish with an extra dollop of soy yogurt, slivered leeks, and fresh watercress.

Yield: 4 servings

SEED CAKE

8 tablespoons (1 stick) Earth Balance, softened

¾ cup sugar

2 teaspoons vanilla

6 tablespoons soy or rice milk

2 teaspoons caraway seeds

1¼ cups flour

2 tablespoons soy flour

3 tablespoons cornstarch

I teaspoon baking powder

I teaspoon cinnamon

¼ teaspoon nutmeg

¼ teaspoon salt

About 2 tablespoons confectioners' sugar for dusting (optional)

This dainty cake was created in England during the Middle Ages. Biting into the caraway seeds feels somewhat unusual, both in terms of flavor and in texture, but take a sip of strong tea first, then it will all make sense. It's really a perfect food pairing.

1. Preheat the oven to 350°F. Grease a 9-inch cake pan.
2. In a large bowl, cream together Earth Balance and sugar. Add vanilla, soy or rice milk, and caraway seeds.
3. In a large bowl, sift together the flours, cornstarch, baking powder, spices, and salt. Fold the dry mixture into wet ingredients, a bit at a time, using a heavy spoon.
4. Spoon the mixture into the cake pan and bake for about 75 minutes, or until a cake tester comes out clean. Let cool for about 10 minutes on a wire rack, then turn out onto a serving plate. Dust with confectioners' sugar, if desired.

Yield: 6–8 servings

EARL GREY COOKIES

Bergamot is the pronounced citrus flavor that perfumes Earl Grey tea. The tea leaves infuse these shortbreads with the same orangey essence, but in a subtle, elegant manner. These cookies are a tea party must, and Earl Grey is only the beginning. Use this recipe as inspiration to make cookies with other pronounced scented teas, like green tea and chai.

2 cups flour
⅔ cup sugar
⅓ cup confectioners' sugar, plus more for dusting
2½ tablespoons Earl Grey tea leaves, finely chopped (from about 3 tea bags)
¼ teaspoon salt
1 teaspoon vanilla
1 cup (2 sticks) Earth Balance, room temperature
½ teaspoon orange or lemon extract (optional, but nice)

1. In a large bowl, combine flour, sugars, tea, and salt. Add remaining ingredients and mix with a beater until a dough forms. Using your hands, press it into a ball, gathering up any rogue dough bits, and divide in half. Roll each piece into a 2-inch log. Wrap tightly in plastic wrap or waxed paper and refrigerate for at least 1 hour.
2. Preheat the oven to 375°F. Grease two cookie sheets well or line them with Silpats.
3. Slice each log into circles ¼- to ⅓-inch thick. Place on cookie sheets, keeping in mind that cookies will spread as they bake.
4. Bake about 10 minutes, or until edges are golden. Let cool for a few minutes, then carefully use a spatula and transfer cookies to wire racks to cool completely.

Yield: 5–6 dozen cookies

SLUMBER PARTY

Spending the night with girlfriends and peeking into each others' home lives is not just an important part of growing up; it's also a bona fide bonding ritual, when young female friends open up and share secrets, snacks, and belly laughs. Slumber parties were one of the highlights of my childhood; I still remember sleepovers on Pam's patio when we played penny poker until dawn.

These recipes are fairly simple, so depending on the ages of the "sleepies," you can leave the girls to their own (albeit, well-guided) devices or you can prep the food for them ahead of time.

MENU: SLEEPY TREATS

1 teaspoon white vinegar

½ cup soy or rice milk

1½ pounds seitan nuggets (about 2-inch pieces)

4 cups cornflakes

1 teaspoon paprika or smoked paprika

½ teaspoon garlic powder

½ teaspoon onion powder

½ teaspoon cumin

Dash of salt

CORNFLAKE-SEITAN NUGGETS

I know I'm going to hear it for this one, but I think a supreme act of parental love is to (occasionally, not habitually) let your kids make a meal based on store-bought breakfast cereal. Although adults and gourmands may initially turn their nose up at this recipe's "trashy factor," the taste of these crispy little nuggets will eventually win them over. (I try not to take myself too seriously!) Best of all, if you use all-natural cornflakes, this recipe is also relatively healthy. Serve with Agave-Mustard Dressing (see page 162), Cumin-Harissa Dipping Sauce (see page 166), or plain old ketchup.

1. Stir the vinegar into the milk. Set aside and let curdle for 5 to 10 minutes. Pour in a shallow tray and add seitan; stir to coat well. Let marinate for 2 hours or overnight.
2. Preheat oven to 375°F. Spray a large cookie sheet with cooking spray.
3. Place remaining ingredients in food processor and whiz until almost powdery. Pour this mixture into a shallow dish and roll each piece of seitan in it to coat. Place on cookie sheet.
4. Bake for 15 minutes or until golden, turning once halfway through.

Yield: 8 servings

15-MINUTE ICE CREAM PIE

This modular recipe is great for any occasion, especially when you're pressed for time. But ice cream and slumber parties are natural counterparts. If you use a store-bought no-bake cookie or graham cracker crust, you can call this recipe "5-Minute Ice Cream Pie." The possibilities truly are endless.

1. Mix all crust ingredients in a large bowl and press into a 9-inch pie pan.
2. Spread softened ice cream into prepared shell. Cover and freeze for 2 hours or until hardened.
3. Decorate the cake with your topping(s) of choice.
4. Soften at room temperature for about 15 minutes before serving.

Variations

For a "parfait" effect, choose 2 different but compatible flavors and layer them in the shell, one at a time, in step 2, allowing the first layer to set in the freezer about 1 hour before spreading on the second later. Here are some flavor combination ideas:

Chocolate and vanilla in a chocolate crust garnished with shaved chocolate curls

Strawberry and banana with fresh strawberries

Dulce de leche and chocolate in a chocolate crust with caramel topping and toasted hazelnuts

Cookie dough and chocolate in a graham cracker crust topped with crumbled vegan Oreo-type cookies

Cherry vanilla and vanilla in a graham cracker crust with vegan whipped cream

Rum raisin and caramel in a graham cracker crust with caramel sauce

Mint chocolate chip and chocolate in a chocolate crust with chocolate sprinkles

Quick Crust

1½ cups finely ground graham cracker crumbs or finely ground chocolate, lemon, ginger, or vanilla wafer cookie crumbs

⅓ cup sugar

6 tablespoons (¾ stick) Earth Balance, melted

2 pints soy, coconut milk, or rice ice cream, softened at room temperature for ½ hour

Toppings: ground and/or toasted nuts, sprinkles, chocolate or caramel sauce, fresh fruit (strawberries, raspberries), chocolate candies, pretzels, shaved chocolate or vegan white chocolate, chocolate chips, vegan whipped cream

POP-ART TARTS

Tart Dough

½ cup (1 stick) Earth Balance, softened

1 cup sugar

1 teaspoon vanilla

4 cups unbleached all-purpose flour

1 heaping tablespoon soy flour

2 teaspoons cream of tartar

¾ teaspoon baking soda

½ teaspoon salt

½ cup soy or rice milk

Chocolate Filling*

6 tablespoons Earth Balance, softened

3 tablespoons Dutch-process cocoa

¾ cup sugar

Pinch of salt

Brown Sugar and Cinnamon Filling*

6 tablespoons Earth Balance, softened

3 tablespoons unbleached all-purpose flour

¾ cup brown sugar

1½ teaspoons cinnamon

Pinch of salt

Fruit Filling*

1¼ cup thick fruit jam (e.g., apricot, raspberry, blueberry)

¼ cup unbleached all-purpose flour

Pinch of salt

Apple Pie Filling*

1¼ cup canned, sweetened apple pie filling

¼ cup unbleached all-purpose flour

1 teaspoon cinnamon

Pinch of salt

When I saw this recipe in my *King Arthur Flour Baker's Companion*, I immediately translated it to vegan—and played around with the filling options. These are as much fun to make as they are to eat for breakfast. It's best to make the tart dough ahead of time. If the girls (or boys) are old enough, they can roll out and assemble these toaster pastries under adult supervision the night of the party. If they are younger, then they can at least decorate the tarts, hence the name "Pop-Art Tarts." This recipe is a bit time consuming, but the end result is worth it. It's best to pick only one or two fillings to try.

1. For the dough, cream together the Earth Balance, sugar, and vanilla in a large bowl. Add the flours, cream of tartar, baking soda, and salt, a bit at a time, alternating with splashes of milk. Scrape down the sides of the mixer as needed. Cover with plastic wrap and refrigerate for a few hours, or ideally overnight.

2. Choose a filling flavor and mix all ingredients in a small bowl until well blended and no lumps remain.

3. Preheat oven to 350°F.

4. Divide the dough into 4 pieces and, on a Silpat or lightly floured surface, roll out 1 section into a rectangle approximately 12 x 8 inches and as thin as you can manage, about ¹⁄₁₆ inch. Cut into 3 x 4-inch rectangles, and place on a lightly greased or Silpat-lined cookie sheet. Repeat with another quarter of the dough; keep the remaining 2 dough sections in the fridge.

5. Spread about 1 tablespoon filling on top of these rectangles. Be sure to leave a ⅛-inch border unfilled so you can pinch the edges together.

6. Roll and cut out the remaining dough and place on top of the filled rectangles. Seal the edges all the way around each tart with a fork, then prick air holes all across the top of each tart so the steam can escape.

7. Bake tarts for about 20 minutes, or until golden brown. Remove from oven and cool on racks.

8. For the icing, add 2 tablespoons milk and vanilla to confectioners' sugar. Whisk until smooth. If the icing seems too thick, add more milk, in 1 teaspoon increments, until it reaches a thick but spreadable consistency. Color the frosting, if desired, and spread on top of the cooled tarts. Decorate, if desired. Let cool, and then toast!

Yield: 16 tarts

Icing

1½ cups confectioners' sugar

2–3 tablespoon soy or rice milk

¼ teaspoon vanilla

Food coloring (see Nature's Food Coloring, page 29)

Optional Decorations

Colored sugar

Sprinkles

* Each filling recipe makes enough to fill 16 tarts, so halve or quarter the recipes, depending on how many you want to try.

ENDURANCE EVENT

Never mind winning. Anyone who has had the courage to train for a marathon or half marathon, duathalon, triathlon, long-distance cycling race, or the holy grail of athletics—the Ironman—knows that just finishing is the true reason to celebrate. If you know someone who is completing a milestone event, why not fete them both pre- and postrace?

MENU: ATHLETE'S FOOD

Before the Event: Prerace Carb Load
PASTA WITH RED PEPPERS AND BASIL

This dish is easy to make, but it's time intensive because of all the chopping and stirring that's involved. That's exactly why I find making this pasta meditative, a good state of mind to be in the night before an important race.

1. Bring a large pot of salted water to boil for the pasta.
2. In a large, high-sided pan, heat oil over medium-low heat. Add garlic and red pepper flakes and sauté very slowly, taking extra care not to burn the garlic, until garlic is very soft, about 10 minutes. The idea here is to infuse the oil with the heat from the garlic and pepper.
3. Add sliced red peppers. Turn heat to medium and sauté, stirring every few minutes. The peppers will exude liquid; this is fine, keep stirring. When the liquid is reabsorbed, add a tablespoon or two of the broth. (If you're using a nonstick pan, adding broth may not be necessary.) Continue stirring and cooking the peppers very slowly, until they are quite soft and flavorful, about 20 minutes. Start cooking pasta about halfway through.
4. Add basil and lemon zest to pasta and toss. Drain pasta very well, shaking colander to remove excess water.
5. Toss pasta with pepper mixture. Top with pine nuts and drizzle with extra oil, if desired. Adjust seasonings and top with nutritional yeast.

Yield: 6–8 servings

1 pound pasta (gemelli, farfalle, rotini, or penne rigate)

4 tablespoons extra-virgin olive oil, plus extra for drizzling (optional)

10 cloves garlic, sliced (yes, you read right)

¼ teaspoon red pepper flakes

2 pounds organic red bell peppers, thinly sliced (about 9 small peppers)

Up to ½ cup vegetable broth

½ cup chopped fresh basil

Zest of 1 lemon

½ cup pine nuts, toasted

Salt and pepper to taste

Nutritional yeast for topping

Wine Pairing
The lemon and basil here suggest
a crisp, herbaceous Trebbiano d'Abbruzzo.

1 cup creamy natural peanut
  butter
¾ cup agave nectar
2¾ cups rolled oats
¼ cup ground flaxseed
1 teaspoon cinnamon
Pinch of salt

During the Event
No-Bake Energy Bars

You're on mile fifteen of your grueling twenty-mile training run and you're hitting the wall. One of these tasty bars will give you a needed hit of energy, thanks to the sugar and carbs, plus a shot of salt to replenish what you lost while sweating. They're also rich in omega-3s.

1. Spray a 9 x 9-inch baking dish with cooking spray.
2. In a medium saucepan over medium-low heat, combine peanut butter and agave nectar. Whisk until smooth.
3. Stir in the oats, flaxseed, cinnamon, salt, and any optional additions. Spread into prepared pan. Place in refrigerator to speed cooling.
4. Cut into 16 bars, or into your desired size; some athletes may prefer bite-sized nuggets.

Yield: About 16 bars

Variations
You can also use Chocolate–Peanut Butter Dip, see page 141,
in place of the creamy peanut butter.
Add up to ¼ cup of any of the following:
dried cranberries, raisins, nuts, chocolate chips, crushed banana chips.

Tip
Wrap each bar in plastic wrap. Tuck one or two in your fanny pack or in the pocket of your bike shirt before you embark on your training session.

After the Event
POSTRACE PROTEIN SHAKE

After going through the rigors of an endurance event, it's important to consume some protein immediately after in order to feed your weary muscles and help your body kick-start the recovery process. This yummy protein shake relies on soy for its main protein, with some extra heft and sweet creaminess from the nut butter. It may taste like dessert, but it's good for you. So drink up!

Whiz everything together in a food processor until very smooth.

Yield: 1 shake

1 cup soy milk

1 banana

2 tablespoons unsweetened cocoa powder

2 tablespoons cashew, almond, or peanut butter

4 dates

Agave nectar or maple syrup to taste (optional)

A few ice cubes (add enough to reach your desired consistency)

BUCKEYES

After completing an endurance event, you need to rehydrate—and replenish protein. These peanut butter–based candies will give you a quick shot of energy and protein. The liquor adds a little bit of elegance, but omit it if the athlete does not indulge. Buckeyes supposedly get their name from the dark shiny nuts of the buckeye tree, which look a lot like these tasty little candies.

1. Line cookie sheets with Silpat mats, waxed paper, or parchment paper.
2. Beat peanut butter, Earth Balance, and liquor (if using) together in large bowl until smooth. Beat in confectioners' sugar, about 1 cup at a time, until mixture holds together as dough. Shape into 1-inch balls; place on prepared cookie sheets. Freeze for 1 hour.
3. Melt chips and shortening in medium glass bowl, uncovered, on 50 percent power for 3 minutes; stir. Microwave in additional 10- to 15-second intervals as needed, stirring just until melted.
4. Dip peanut butter balls into melted chocolate using a toothpick. You can a leave small section of the center uncovered or dip the entire "buckeye." Shake off excess chocolate and scrape bottom of candy on side of bowl. Return to baking sheets; refrigerate until chocolate hardens. Store in covered container in refrigerator.

Yield: About 60–80 Buckeyes, depending on how big you make them

2 cups creamy peanut butter

¼ cup (½ stick) Earth Balance, softened

4 tablespoons Kahlua, brandy, or rum (optional)

3¾–4 cups confectioners' sugar

2 cups dark chocolate chips or buttons

2 tablespoons nonhydrogenated vegetable shortening

Variations

For extra-decadent Buckeyes, use the Chocolate–Peanut Butter Dip (see page 141) instead of the peanut butter. You can also substitute cashew, almond, or soy butter for the peanut butter.

SICK DAY

When you're feeling under the weather and life's endless demands all seem to scream for your attention at once, it can be hard enough to take a sick day, let alone to consider it a holiday.

I find that when I resist rest the most, that's when it's truly time to slow down and really *listen* to my body. That's when a sick day morphs into a celebration, albeit a quiet, personal one. A sick day is time to fete your body's innate ability to heal, and your ability to center and nurture yourself—a wonderful lesson to teach your children through your actions. When you're ill, your body wisely abates your appetite, saving its energy for the more important task of healing itself. But still, a few bites of some bland, easy-to-prepare foods are comforting and warming.

MENU: A DAY OF NURTURING

GINGER TEA

2 teaspoons roughly chopped, peeled fresh ginger

1 cup boiling water

2 teaspoons agave nectar or maple syrup, or to taste (or you can sweeten with Stevia)

Fresh lemon, orange, or lime juice to taste (optional)

Upset tummy? Nothing soothes a wonky gut more effectively than a cup of gentle Ginger Tea, which has also been used for centuries across the globe to treat morning sickness. This homemade version is super simple to prepare and costs way less than those too-cool, hipster tea bags.

1. Pour boiling water over ginger. Let steep for about 10 minutes.
2. Strain, sweeten to taste, and add citrus juice, if using.

Yield: 1 cup

MINIMAL PASTINA WITH SPINACH

When I am stuffed up with a bad cold, I crave this easy-to-prepare clear soup. It takes about ten minutes to make from start to finish, and it's gentle on the stomach. I like to use my kitchen scissors to cut the spinach into the soup. Even though chopping the greens is just as easy, there's something defiant about using the scissors, especially when you're not feeling well. Skip the spinach if you're experiencing a GI bug (easier to digest without the veggies).

4 cups vegetable broth
½ cup pastina (or any small pasta like orzo or ditalini)
1 cup spinach, shredded or cut (frozen is fine, too)
Nutritional yeast, salt, and pepper to taste
Splash of lemon juice (optional)

In a large saucepan, bring broth to a boil. Add pasta, lemon juice if desired, and spinach. Cook according to pasta package directions. Adjust seasonings and serve.

Yield: 4 servings

Variations

Use Swiss chard, collards, escarole, or kale instead of spinach.
Add ½ cup of cooked chickpeas, beans, edamame, peas, corn, or cubed tofu.

1 organic apple (any kind but Red or Golden Delicious)

Fillings

Choose 1 of the following fillings, or a mixture:

2 tablespoons raisins

2 tablespoons cranberries

2 tablespoons crushed nuts (preferably toasted)

1 tablespoon brown sugar, maple syrup, or agave nectar

¼ teaspoon cinnamon

Pinch of nutmeg and/or cardamom

2 tablespoons ginger ale or brewed chai tea

Pat of Earth Balance

BAKED APPLES

Sometimes you crave a little sweet, even when you're sick. My mom used to make this dish for me all the time during winter, especially when I wasn't feeling up to snuff. I love the recipe because it's modular and lends itself well to improvisation. If you're making this when you're not sick, you might also consider finishing it off with a healthy scoop of vanilla or dulce de leche soy ice cream. I've listed ingredients for just one baked apple, but you can easily extrapolate, as needed, and make as many as you need. Please use organic apples so you don't have to worry about eating the skin. This is a great dish for kids to help out with.

1. Preheat the oven to 400°F. Lightly coat a baking dish with cooking spray.
2. Core the apple, leaving ½-inch base at the bottom, and scoop out any seeds. Stuff with filling(s) of your choice and top with sweetener of your choice. Dust with cinnamon and nutmeg and/or cardamom. Drizzle with ginger ale or chai and top with a pat of Earth Balance.
3. Bake about 15 to 30 minutes or until apple is soft; time will vary depending on the size of the apple you use. Serve warm.

Yield: 1 serving

Variation

Substitute pears or Asian pears for the apples.

SNOW DAY

Big presentation at work. Your daughter's ballet lesson. The dog's vet appointment. Your mother-in-law's birthday. Suddenly, Mother Nature intervenes and sends down a snowstorm, putting all of life's seemingly important "obligations" to a halt. Schools are closed. The office is closed. Roads are closed. There's nothing to do but watch guilty-pleasure TV, putter around in the kitchen, and catch up on that novel you've been putting off. Now that's a reason to celebrate.

MENU: CABIN FEVER FARE

CINNAMON-DATE SCONES

When I'm snowed in, I instantly feel like languishing over copious cups of tea. It's one of those rare times when I actually have time to make breakfast. Scones always make the day seem a bit special, especially when slathered with Earth Balance and a drizzle of agave nectar.

1. Heat oven to 425°F. Grease a cookie sheet.
2. In a large bowl, mix all dry ingredients except for the dates. Add the Earth Balance chunks to this mixture, and using your fingers, rub well into the flour. The mixture should resemble damp sand. Stir in the dates.
3. In another bowl, mix all the wet ingredients. Add to the flour mixture and mix until just wet. Do not overmix. The dough should be wet, but not too wet, and it will stick to your hands a bit. If it's too dry, add more milk, 1 tablespoon at a time.
4. Form into a ball and place on the greased cookie sheet. Use your fingers to press and form into a 7- to 8-inch round. Cut into 8 wedges but don't separate.
5. Bake for 16 to 18 minutes or until top is golden brown and a knife or cake tester inserted into the thickest part of the scones comes out clean.
6. Remove from oven, retrace your cut lines with a knife, and allow to cool on a rack. Serve plain, with Earth Balance, or with jam or agave, if desired.

Yield: 8 scones

1½ cups flour (I use half spelt and half whole wheat pastry flour)
½ cup sugar
2 heaping tablespoons soy flour
1 tablespoon baking powder
1 teaspoon cinnamon
½ teaspoon sea salt
4 tablespoons (½ stick) cold Earth Balance, cut into pea-size pieces
1 cup chopped dates
½ cup rice milk (plus more to add if the dough is too dry)
1 teaspoon apple cider vinegar
1 teaspoon vanilla extract
Earth Balance, jam, agave nectar for serving (optional)

Variations

Substitute dried blueberries, raisins, or raspberries for the dates.
Add ½ cup toasted, chopped nuts of your choice.

VEGGIE-CENTRIC SEITAN

2 teaspoons coconut or olive oil

⅛–¼ teaspoon red pepper flakes

1 sweet onion, roughly chopped

3 garlic cloves, sliced

2 organic red peppers, chopped

2 carrots, thinly sliced

8 ounces mushrooms, sliced

2 tablespoons dried parsley

1 teaspoon dried thyme

1 teaspoon fennel seeds

½ teaspoon dried sage

1½ cups seitan

Miso broth (1 teaspoon miso dissolved in ¼ cup water)

1 bunch bok choy, sliced (you can substitute green cabbage, but I like the slightly bitter taste of the bok choy)

Simple foods are the best—and most warming. I actually came up with this recipe serendipitously one night, about two days before I was leaving for vacation. The fridge was jam-packed with various sundry veggies and a generous portion of seitan. Determined not to let the food go to waste, I began cooking, tossing everything together and adding seasonings that I knew would make the ingredients get along well. When I stepped in my kitchen that night, I had no intention of writing a formal recipe, but the end result was so tasty that after polishing off two servings, I immediately ran to my computer to write down the recipe before I forgot. You can eat this dish as is, or serve it over pasta, potatoes, or your favorite whole grain.

1. Heat oil in a large nonstick pot over medium heat. Sauté red pepper flakes, onion, and garlic until soft, about 5 minutes.
2. Add the peppers and carrots. Sauté for about 10 minutes, or until peppers start to soften, stirring occasionally.
3. Toss in the mushrooms, dried herbs, and seitan. Cook for about 10 more minutes, stirring occasionally.
4. Toss in the miso broth and bok choy. Stir, cover, and cook for 20 minutes.

Yield: 4 servings

Variations

Add 1 cup of any of the following during step 4: finely chopped broccoli or cauliflower, peas or corn, edamame, or chopped organic spinach.

Wine Pairing

Try a half-dry (halbtrocken) German Riesling from the Mittelrhein. The slate-laden soil lends minerality and a "good funk" that pairs especially well with mushrooms and miso.

PANFORTE

Panforte is like fruit cake on steroids. I love the fact that it's stood the test of time: It dates back to the thirteenth century. Panforte is the perfect recipe to make when you have cabin fever and just feel like puttering about in the kitchen. The name translates to "strong bread," so as you might guess, you only need a small slice. It's delicious served with coffee or tea.

1. Preheat oven to 400°F. Line a springform pan with parchment paper and spray with cooking spray.
2. Spread nuts on a cookie sheet and toast until golden, about 4 minutes. Lower oven heat to 350°F. Put in food processor and chop very finely, but be careful not to grind into a pulp or flour.
3. In a large saucepan, mix sugar and agave nectar over medium heat. Continue cooking until a thread forms when you lift a spoon after stirring, about 8 to 10 minutes. Remove from heat and stir in the nuts and the remaining ingredients with a sturdy spoon—or just use your hands. Spread into the springform pan, smooth the top, and bake for 35 to 40 minutes.
4. Cool on a wire rack, then dust with confectioners' sugar.

Yield: 8–10 servings

2 cups whole blanched almonds

1 cup walnuts

1½ cups confectioners' sugar, plus extra for decoration

½ cup agave nectar

½ cup dried but soft, de-stemmed, and finely chopped Calimyrna figs

1½ cups very finely chopped candied fruit peel

Zest of 1 lemon

Zest of 1 orange

1½ teaspoons cinnamon

½ teaspoon nutmeg

½ teaspoon ground coriander

¼ teaspoon ground cloves

½ teaspoon freshly ground black pepper

⅓ cup Dutch-process cocoa

2 tablespoons flour (any kind will do here)

EASY APPLE TARTS

1 1-pound package vegan puff pastry

2 large, tart apples (like Granny Smiths or Macintosh), peeled, quartered, and cut into slices

4 tablespoons packed brown sugar

1 teaspoon cinnamon

Pinch of salt

4 tablespoons (½ stick) Earth Balance, melted

1 tablespoon canola or coconut oil for glaze

Vegan whipped cream or soy or coconut ice cream (optional)

I enjoy an almost primal sense of comfort when I smell apples and cinnamon wafting from my oven during a fierce winter storm. These little gems convey real elegance for a minimal amount of effort. And eating them is a celebration in itself, especially when crowned with a dollop of vegan whipped cream or soy or coconut ice cream. Most puff pastry is made with butter, but you can find margarine- or oil-based puff pastries at most larger health food stores.

1. Preheat oven to 400°F.
2. Lightly flour a work surface. (I like to work on a Silpat or waxed paper.) Unfold one sheet of puff pastry. Use an 8- or 9-inch tart or pie pan as a template and trace and cut out a circle.
3. Fill the center of the circle with concentric circles of apple slices. You should leave about a 1-inch border of "naked" pastry, since you will roll this up to make the crust.
4. Sprinkle slices with sugar, cinnamon, and a pinch of salt. Pour about 2 teaspoons of melted Earth Balance on top. Fold up the pastry edges to make a crust. Brush the crust with oil. Repeat steps 1–4 seven more times.
5. Place tarts on a large cookie sheet and bake for about 20 to 25 minutes or until apples are bubbly and crust is golden. (It's important to bake them in the center of the oven and not too close to the heat source).

Yield: 8 servings

RAW CELEBRATION

I remember years ago, wondering if the raw foods craze would eventually die off. But thanks to some incredibly inventive chefs, cookbook authors, and restaurateurs, "raw" has caught on like wildfire and is now a bona fide lifestyle. Chances are you have some raw friends. These recipes will celebrate the rawsomeness of eating living foods, whether you're having friends over for a birthday, holiday, or an informal gathering.

MENU: RAWSOME FOODS

ZUCCHINI "LINGUINE" WITH LEMONY SPINACH PESTO

This is a gorgeous entree to serve—green and white curls of zucchini pasta, punctuated with fire engine–red pepper flecks and an intense green mound of pesto. And it has substance as well as style: a slightly sweet spinach pesto with just a nudge of sour coating the freshest, healthiest pasta you've ever tasted. Plus you don't need to worry about whether it's al dente; raw pasta never gets overcooked. I'll be the first to admit it: I don't eat as much raw food as I should, but I could eat this dish every day. Using a spiral slicer to make the pasta is your best bet. (They're available in most gourmet shops and online.) But patient, skilled chefs can hand-cut noodles from zucchini. It's also best to let the "linguine" pasta drain as long as possible, at least 8 hours.

1. Toss all pesto ingredients into food processor and process until smooth.
2. Divide zucchini "pasta" among four plates, and top each with red pepper flecks, and ¼ of the pesto.

Yield: 4 servings

Pesto
2 cups packed organic baby spinach leaves
¼ cup raw almonds
1 teaspoon soy sauce
3 tablespoons cold-pressed extra-virgin olive oil
Juice of 1 lemon (about 2 tablespoons)
Zest of 1 lemon
Sea salt to taste

1 large zucchini, cut into spaghetti-like strands and drained in a colander for at least 8 hours (I suggest doing this before you leave for work)
½ organic red pepper, very thinly sliced into 1- or 2-inch "flecks"

TWEAK YOUR 'TUDE
If you're just dipping your toes into the raw food waters and are having trouble considering this recipe as an entree, then try it as a salad.

1 cup hazelnuts
½ cup dates plus 1 cup dates,
  pitted
3 tablespoons water
1 tablespoon raw agave nectar
¼ cup raw cacao powder
  (available in the raw food aisle of
  most large health food stores),
  plus extra for dusting (optional)
¼ teaspoon cinnamon

TRUFFLE-STUFFED DATES

1. Mix hazelnuts, ½ cup dates, water, agave nectar, cacao powder, and cinnamon in food processor until smooth.
2. Using a demitasse spoon, spoon the mixture into the remaining 1 cup dates. Dust with extra cacao powder, if desired.

Yield: About 1 dozen, depending on the size of the dates

Hint

The paste made in step 1 also makes a great tart base for raw fruit tarts—just press it into a mini tart pan. It's a good use for any leftover paste from this recipe.

1 apple
½-inch piece peeled fresh ginger
½ small red beet
8 carrots
¼ lemon

RUBY RED COCKTAIL

Ever since I sipped a fantastic ruby-red juice at Bob's Juice Bar in Paris (www.bobsjuicebar.com) last year, I have been obsessed with trying to replicate it. This is my best attempt. I love the juxtaposition of heat from the ginger against the sweetness of the carrots, apple, and beet. The lemon adds just a tiny bit of balancing pucker. You need a juicer for this recipe.

If you want the real deal, please go see Bob. I admit his is way better. You will have to stand in line, but trust me, the juice and the food are worth the wait.

Process everything in your juicer. Serve on ice or at room temperature.

Yield: 1 large drink

Acknowledgments

Thank you . . .

My family: Regina Grunwalski, Genia Shea, Barbara Byorick, Debbie Post, nieces, nephews, and grand-nieces and grand-nephews. Thank you for always being there for me, in the good times and the bad. Love and cherish you.

Paul: Incredible photographer and artist, environmentalist, professor, visionary. I feel so lucky we found each other, and I appreciate and cherish every minute we spend together. Love you, Sweetheart. XOXO

BFFs: Lisa Larson, Pam Sweeney, Violet Philips, Claire Nixon.

Dear Friends: Ann and Tim Duffield, Cathy Walter, Virginie Péan, Fredrik Faïth. Thanks for the continued love and encouragement.

The French Vegan Connection: Deborah, Alexandre, and Caroline Pivain and Aurelia D'Andrea—Thanks for inviting me to participate in Paris Vegan Day and for getting the word out in France about my books. Bisous!

Facebook and Twitter friends and fans: Thanks for the positivity and the laughs!

Ursula Augustine of Ursula's About PHace: Thanks for the positivity and the fabulous vegan makup for the back-cover photo.

Testers: I am forever grateful. This is *our* book. Hugs to Tara Barnes, Monika Soria Caruso, Stephanie Dana, Rob Branch-Dasch, Catherine "Kip" Dorrell, Bethany R. Fehlinger, Vicki Hodge, Carrie Bagnell Horsburgh, Karissa Johnson, Natalie Kenis, Jenny Moffatt, Shelly-Dawn Moquet, Andréa and Rich Nichols, Stephanie Pelser, Valerie Oula, Jacob Randolph, Constanze Reichardt, Sara Rose, The Selfish Vegan, Jackie Smith, Leinana Two Moons, Bill and Sunnie Watson, Liz Wyman, Bahar Zaker, Andrea Zeichner.

Sommelier and friend: Susan Crawshaw of Moore Brothers Wine. Thanks for the excellent Wine Pairings!

My agent: Clare Pelino.

GLOSSARY

Agave nectar: Sweetener made from the agave plant. Excellent substitute for honey.

Instant vital wheat gluten: Pure protein extracted from the wheat kernel. This powder is used to make seitan and to help bread rise.

Nutritional yeast: Cheesy, nutty tasting yeast prized for its nutrition.

Seitan: "Wheat meat" made from wheat gluten. Very chewy and absorbs marinades and sauces well.

Shoyu: A soy sauce made from soy beans that have been fermented. The flavor is distinct and much more robust then generic soy sauces.

Sumac: Middle Eastern herb with faint lemon undertones.

Tahini: Sesame seed butter, typically used in Middle Eastern foods.

Teff: A tiny grain that hails from Ethiopia, famous for its slightly sour flavor. Teff is famously used to make *injera* bread.

Tempeh: Fermented soybean cakes common in Indonesian food.

Tofu: Pressed soybean "cheese." Neutral flavor; absorbs whatever flavoring you impart it with.

TVP (Textured vegetable protein): TVP is made from soy flour after the soybean oil has been extracted, then cooked under pressure, extruded, and dried. It has a "meaty" texture, similar to ground beef.

ADDITIONAL RESOURCES

Vegan Online Shops
Online supply shops (Groceries, pastries, staples, etc)

Vegan Essentials
veganessentials.com

Food Fight
foodfightgrocery.com

Cosmo's Vegan Shoppe
cosmosveganshoppe.com

Viva Granola (Canada)
vivagranolaveganstore.ca

Cool vegan shoes and accessories
Moo Shoes
mooshoes.com

Cool Websites

Girly Girl Army (Glamazon guide to green living)
girliegirlarmy.com

The Discerning Brute
thediscerningbrute.com
Vegan food, fashion & etiquette for the ethically handsome man

Vegan Worldwide Restaurant Locator
Happy Cow
happycow.net

Vegan Alcohol Check
Barnivore
barnivore.com

RECIPE INDEX BY CATEGORY

Drinks
Alcoholic

Nonalcoholic

Entrees

Pies

RECIPE INDEX

ABOUT THE AUTHOR

Dynise Balcavage is the author of *The Urban Vegan: 250 Simple, Sumptuous Recipes, from Street-Cart Favorites to Haute Cuisine* and eleven books for young readers. She has published recipes in *VegNews*, the *Philadelphia Daily News, Herbivore,* and *Végétariens* (France's first vegetarian magazine) and has been interviewed for the *New York Times,* the *International Herald Tribune,* and *Vegetarian Times.* She's done vegan cooking demonstrations from New York to Paris. When she's not globe-trotting, Dynise lives in Philadelphia with her three cats, all former strays. She tweets at the urbanvegan and blogs at urbanvegan.net.